Praise for *The Barefoot Investor*

This book will help you protect the people you love.

—**Melissa Doyle, host of** *Sunday Night*

Scott is one of the best communicators on financial matters in Australia—in fact, one of the best communicators full stop. More importantly, what he writes not only makes common sense, it's correct and has integrity. He's a commentator with no axe to grind (apart from the one at his farm), and there aren't many of us.

—**Alan Kohler, ABC Finance Presenter,** *Constant Investor*

In this book you will read true accounts from a divorcee road train driver, a young widow and a returned defence officer—all of whom have 'gone Barefoot' and are massively better for the experience. They join thousands who are following the Barefoot strategies and are happier, more confident and, importantly, wealthier.

—**Tim Fischer, Former Deputy Prime Minister**

I have always enjoyed reading and listening to Scott talk about money. He is my sort of money guy as he talks in a language we can all understand. More importantly he speaks the truth about money. There are, barring a miracle Lotto win, few shortcuts to wealth, it takes time and effort. This book can really help you to take control of your money. Scott's no-nonsense style is easy to read and he provides a step-by-step guide that will give readers a path to financial security.

—**Paul Clitheroe AM, Chairman Australian Government**
Financial Literacy Board

Why is this the #1 book I recommend to anyone who wants to invest in financial freedom? Because it is much more than just another money book. Scott provides a framework, great ideas and compelling writing to bring to life practical strategies that will truly allow the reader to tread their own path—to achieve financial security, live a purposeful life and leave a lasting legacy.

—**Arun Abey, co-author of** *How Much Is Enough?*

Scott Pape has delivered on a promise often made but rarely kept: this is useful, inspiring and practical advice. His story about the apple tree is worth the entire cost of the book.

—**Seth Godin, bestselling author of** *Linchpin: Are You Indispensable?*

The barefoot investor

The barefoot investor

— THE ONLY MONEY GUIDE —
YOU'LL EVER NEED

SCOTT PAPE

WILEY

First published in 2017 by John Wiley & Sons Australia, Ltd
42 McDougall St, Milton Qld 4064
Office also in Melbourne

Reprinted with updates June 2018

Typeset in 9.75/14 pt Caecilia LT Std

© Barefoot Investment Management Pty Ltd 2017

Illustrations © Jeffrey D Phillips 2017

The moral rights of the author have been asserted

National Library of Australia Cataloguing-in-Publication data:

Creator:	Pape, Scott, 1978- author.
Title:	The Barefoot Investor: the only money guide you'll ever need / Scott Pape.
ISBN:	9780730324218 (pbk.)
	9780730324225 (ebook)
Notes:	Includes index.
Subjects:	Finance, Personal—Australia—Handbooks, manuals, etc.
	Saving and investment—Australia—Handbooks, manuals, etc.
Dewey Number:	332.024

Cover design by Hyungtak Jun
Cover image by Isamu Sawa

The author and publisher would like to thank the following copyright holders, organisations and individuals for their permission to reproduce copyright material in this book: © ING Bank: **p.18**; © Australian Securities and Investments Commission: **p.27**; © Rob Hill / Getty Images Australia: **p.51**; © piranka / Getty Images: **p.51**; © Pacific Brands: **p.55** & **p.56**; © champja / Getty Images: **p.62**; © AAP Image/Dan Peled: **p.138**; © Australian Foundation Investment Company Limited: **p.174**; © Pacific International Music / Lyrics by Garry Koehler: **p.242**.

Printed in Australia by Ligare Book Printer

F007699_071318

Disclaimer

For Liz.
Home is wherever I'm with you.

She leaned in, gently put her hand on mine, and said, 'Honey, I know it will be difficult for you, but you're going to need to let people help you. You've got a young wife, a little baby... and you've just lost everything you own. I'm a financial counsellor. I help people in crisis. Let me help you.'

10 per cent of all author royalties are donated to the not-for-profit financial counselling peak body, Financial Counselling Australia.

Contents

Welcome to the 2018–2019 update

G'day!

Welcome to the 2018 update of *The Barefoot Investor: The Only Money Guide You'll Ever Need*.

This little book began life on my family farm, and morphed into a monster …

It's now sold 1 million copies … and it's become one of the bestselling Australian books of all time.

(My English teacher is still shaking his head in disbelief.)

Along the way it's attracted attention as high up as the Prime Minister.

(I gave him a copy to pass on to the Treasurer … he needs all the help he can get.)

Journalist Monique Bowley described it as 'The Biggest Finance Cult in Australia'. Here's how she put it on Mamamia:

> As I pulled my bank card out of my wallet and scanned the PayPass, the cashier gave me a knowing smile.
> 'You're one of them,' she said. 'Barefoot.'
> I nodded back, slightly embarrassed.
> My cult status was exposed. 'I'm on it too,' she confided. 'And I see it almost every day.'
> Right now, thousands of Australians are flashing orange bank cards with mantras penned on with sharpies and stickers. 'Splurge', they read. 'Daily Expenses', read others.
> And they all signal one thing: that you're following the biggest finance cult in Australia.

Of course one person's cult is another's person's community — but whatever you call it, we're certainly making an impact.

So why am I updating the book?

Well, I plan on doing it each year. See, while the wealth-building principles I write about never change, each year the politicians (and banks) meddle with things.

So I've updated for tax changes, Kim Kardashian's net worth, and retirement figures for the coming financial year.

You're in for a real treat. Kick off your shoes, and welcome to the 'cult'.

Scott Pape
Family Farm
June 2018

No funny stuff, just money stuff

The Barefoot Investor holds an Australian Financial Services Licence (AFSL no. 302081). This book outlines general advice only. It should not replace individual, independent, personal financial advice.

Neither Scott Pape, the Barefoot Investor nor anyone associated with the making of this book has received any kickbacks, commissions or fees—or even so much as an invite to a corporate box at the footy—for recommending or mentioning anything contained herein. We never have, and we never will.

We are *fiercely independent*.

The bottom line: you're reading the same advice that I'd give to my mum, God love her.

About the author

Scott Pape is the founder of the Barefoot Investor.

For well over a decade he's reached millions of Australians through his national weekend newspaper columns, appearances on TV and radio and his bestselling first book.

In 2010 independent research firm CoreData found that:

> Scott Pape is considered the most knowledgeable regarding financial matters, topping the ratings in the areas of superannuation, investment, taxation, insurance and economics. Pape is also considered the most trustworthy, truthful in how he presents himself and in touch with financial matters that affect everyday Australians.

In 2014 he was chosen to assist with the government's national financial literacy in schools program. He has worked with AFL and NRL teams, struggling single mums and elderly pensioners.

The Barefoot Investor's *Barefoot Blueprint* has grown to become one of Australia's largest independent wealth-building communities.

Scott lives in country Victoria with his wife Liz and their three children on their family farm and is often seen belting around in an old ute that doesn't need to be locked.

Prelude: Living Barefoot

A blackened sheep stopped right in the middle of the road and eyeballed us.

Its feet were badly burnt. It was shaking. The wool on its side was scorched into curly knots, revealing its bloodied ribcage. It was heaving in and out, clutching for air. In shock. Dehydrated. Traumatised.

With our fences destroyed, the poor girl was left stumbling around on her own, searching for water on our home block. Most of her flock had been burnt alive when a bushfire ripped through my farm 24 hours earlier.

Bang...Bang...*Bang*.

Without my knowledge or approval, the Department of Environment and Primary Industries had rolled up at first light and begun destroying my surviving sheep. Apparently they can do that when your farm is declared part of a disaster zone.

The sheep limped off to the side of the road. They'd find her soon.

I gripped my wife Liz's hand and continued driving down our driveway towards our family home.

Two chimneys and a pile of rubble were the sum total of a lifetime of possessions.

Her wedding dress. Tea cups. The few last remaining photos of her late father, who had died 10 years earlier. Butter knives. All of my baby son's clothes. All of his toys. Everything was gone.

Overhead, a TV news chopper hovered. Later, it would land amid our dead and dying animals, and a reporter would enter what remained of our private family home and kick through the still-smouldering personal possessions that had made our little family us.

At the time I was used to fronting the nightly finance news; that day I was the news.

With the thick smell of everything burning, the sight of everything we'd worked for in ashes and a chopper buzzing around us, my wife erupted. She began screaming uncontrollably. Deep, loud groans of pain. Our baby son, who was strapped in his car seat, began bawling in sympathy.

At that moment, when everything was falling apart, I looked in the rear-view mirror and said to myself the first thing that came to my mind:

'I've got this.'

That's the truth. That's exactly what I said. Don't get me wrong: I'm not some Bruce Willis diehard tough-guy character. Far from it. But if this was the lowest point in my life, there was something deep inside of me that knew I could handle it.

And over the next two years, I did.

The belly of this book came from that one moment.

Because here's the thing: at some stage you're going to face your own financial fire.

It could be when your partner walks out on you and the kids.

It could be when you're sitting alone in the work carpark after the boss has made you redundant.

It could be after you go to the doctor for a simple 'check-up'.

It could be your girlfriend telling you she's pregnant.

It could be when you glance at your super statement and wonder how you'll ever afford to retire.

No matter what you face in the future, I want you to be able to look yourself in the eye and confidently say to yourself:

I've got this.

And by the end of this book, that's exactly what you'll be able to do.

Plant, Grow, Harvest

After the fire, we looked at the devastation that surrounded us, and were totally overwhelmed.

The smell gets into your lungs...into your brain.

The day before, we had a 'to do' list. Now we had a phone book.

With a million things to do, where would we even start?

Well, we chose to...plant a tree.

An apple tree.

It wasn't a short-term fix, obviously.

After all, you don't plant an apple tree on a Saturday and then come back on Sunday and stand with your hands on your hips and scowl:

'Where are my freaking apples?'

No, you don't do that.

You don't pull out the sapling a week later and replant it on the other side of the yard where you think it's (maybe) sunnier.

You don't stay up at night worrying that your golden retriever is threatening to lift its leg on the trunk.

You don't nervously watch the weather on the nightly news and think to yourself, 'There's no rain on the five-day forecast! El Niño will wipe out everything. This is a disaster!'

You don't get desperate and google 'How to grow a thousand apples a day, with one tree'.

No, you just plant the bloody tree.

And then you wait.

A year or so later it bears some apples (mostly hard, small and sour). Its branches are still young, so the weight of the apples makes it droopy. (It looks like a tree version of a fashion model.)

And then you basically forget about it, and get on with your life.

You trust that the tree will grow, and that it will get all it needs from the rain, the sun and the nutrients in the soil. The exact same way trees have been growing since Adam and Eve shacked up and did the wild thing.

And a few more years go by, and then one day you walk past the tree and notice it's now a few metres tall and there are a few really juicy, ripe apples just waiting to be picked.

And then 30 years go by, and that little sapling has transformed into a big, beautiful tree with thick, strong branches that you attach a rope to as a swing for your grandkids to play on. And the apples feed your entire family.

And when you're long gone, your grandkids' kids still play under that magnificent old tree.

Nature has an easy-to-understand pattern: plant, grow and harvest.

It's the same with your money.

In this book, we're going to follow the same natural pattern.

We'll plant the seeds of wealth.

We'll watch them grow.

And then, we'll enjoy a life-changing harvest.

Let's begin.

The alpaca attitude

Friends of ours moved to the country and bought a family home on a two-acre block.

They had so much space that they thought it would be nice to buy their kids a couple of alpacas. You know, to give them a real taste of the country life. The kids even gave them names: Alberto and Pedro.

Truth is, buying alpacas as pets is like taking heroin for a headache: they're basically camels without humps, and with the aggression of Tony Abbott.

Alberto and Pedro lived in the family's front yard.

The problem with that location is that alpacas are protectors by nature, so they naturally felt it was their responsibility to protect the family from any 'predators' that might approach the front gate—like the postie, family friends with small children, or grandparents.

Seriously, you'd walk up to their gate minding your own business, and then ... *Bam!* Out of nowhere, two surly, six-foot-five alpacas would be charging at you. *Whoosh!* They'd swing up on their hind legs, cock their heads to the side and ... *Hoick!* They'd shower you with green spit.

It was totally out of control.

So one day, over a cuppa, my wife offered to take them to our farm.

There was method to her madness. We'd already lost a number of our lambs that season to foxes, so the idea was to put the alpacas in with a flock of sheep and let the foxes know to keep the hell away—or they risked getting stomped.

Good plan.

I dutifully borrowed a horse float from a neighbour and drove to our friends' home to pick up Alberto and Pedro—only to find that things were already out of hand.

The 40-something father had Alberto in a headlock and was attempting to frogmarch him down the driveway.

It was two against one.

Pedro was darting around, shrieking at the top of his voice, violently headbutting him.

'The kids are really going to ... *don't you bloody spit on me!* ... miss them,' he panted.

The kids were inside the house playing games, oblivious to the fact that their dad was copping repeated kicks to the kidneys.

Fast-forward to the day after the fires.

As we left the remains of our destroyed home, I looked across a burnt-out paddock and saw Alberto and Pedro circling protectively around a small flock of burnt, traumatised sheep.

The alpacas' hooves were so badly burned they were having trouble standing. They'd collapse to the ashen ground and then stoically lurch back up, groaning in pain. The Department was trying to destroy the sheep—but Alberto and Pedro wouldn't let them.

No-one messes with their flock.

Nothing was going to stop them. Not being burnt. Not struggling to stand. Not staring down the barrel of a rifle. They didn't flinch. They didn't take a backward step. That was their job. That was their purpose.

How's that for focus?

I want you to think about your money exactly the same way.

See, after years of doing this, I can already tell who's going to make it—the people who have that same *alpaca attitude* when it comes to their money.

It's easy to spot them. They say things like, 'Okay, so we're just going to have to work our arses off until we're debt free' or 'I can't afford to run this car, so I'll sell it and buy something cheaper'.

These people don't know it yet, but they're already free: *free* from excuses, *free* from second-guessing themselves and *free* from constantly worrying about their financial future. That's the payoff for standing up, making a decision and taking responsibility for your situation.

But most people aren't alpacas—they're groundhogs.

They do the same thing day in, day out... and then bitch and moan that 'nothing ever changes'.

Case in point: currently I have more than 13 000 money questions in my inbox. At a glance I can tell which ones are sent by the groundhogs (most of them). They ask questions like, 'So I've been thinking about learning about day trading' or 'I can't pay my bills... should I just go bankrupt :(?'

Groundhogs want the magic diet shake rather than the daily 5am run.

And that's why, for most people, five years ago looks pretty much the same as today... with a few nicer clothes—but with the same excuses, the same regrets and more debt.

Here's the deal: the goal of the Barefoot Investor can be summarised in one word: *control*.

I'm going to provide you with a set of steps that will give you control over your money and your life.

It will work for you, just as it has for thousands of others.

But it ain't easy.

It's not enough to skim through this book and think about opening a few accounts. If it were, everyone would be rich.

I'm deadly serious when I say this: if you want financial freedom, you need to take charge. And, just like an alpaca, you have to be prepared to stand up and fight like your life depends on it—and never, ever back down.

Put your foot down

The first person you need to fight is yourself.

Picture what you looked like in your high-school photo.

If you were anything like me, you were awkward, gangly and so ashamed of your braces you didn't open your mouth (though you now *thank Christ* your old man made you get them).

Even though we're now older, possibly partnered up, and have visible veins on our legs and hair growing out of our ears, deep down we're all still only a few shades from that insecure little kid.

But here's the important part: that kid in the picture formed a lot of beliefs and assumptions about who you are and what you're capable of.

And the problem is that decades roll by and life gets busy, and if no-one challenges the negative 'scripts' that auto-play in your head whenever you stuff something up or get rejected, those teenage beliefs bed down, compound and become ingrained—they become who you are.

And they slowly but surely eat away at your self-confidence, keeping you locked in a job you've lost interest in, relationships you've outgrown and a financial state that stops you from experiencing life on your terms.

Believe me, as a finance guy, I've seen it thousands of times.

It's like a mate of mine who's an awesome mechanic. I've watched him turn his head to the side and listen as a car pulls up, and casually tell the driver, 'Time to tighten your fan-belt cobber... and get them to change the oil while they're at it'. To me, he's like the Nostradamus of cars. For him, it's nothing special; it's just what he does: after years of doing something day in, day out, patterns emerge that are easy to pick.

It's the same with my job. The best way to get to the guts of someone's financial situation (other than poring over their financials) is to turn my head, and listen intently as they describe their situation.

Patterns always emerge. Here are some of the scripts that may be turning over in your financial fanbelt right now.

> **Here's you:** I'm not that smart with money.

> **Here's me:** No-one is born 'smart with money'. It's a learnt skill—like driving—and it has more to do with your behaviour than your brains. This explains why I know a lot of so-called financial experts who don't have two bob to rub together—and why I also know wealthy people who never finished high school. You don't need to be a financial expert to win with money. It's much more important to start than it is to be smart. And remember: you're in luck—you've got me as your independent tour guide to financial independence.

> **Here's you:** I don't earn enough.

> **Here's me:** It's not about what you earn, but what you save. I've had clients who were cleaners their entire lives, who never earned more than the minimum wage, but used compound interest to build a million-dollar portfolio.

> **Here's you:** I've left it too late…I should have saved more when I was younger.

> **Here's me:** Stop for a second and tell me what age you'll be when you die.

Go on…answer that.

I'll wait.

Most people don't think about their long-term future, but nearly everyone has a specific age in mind when they'll die.

Next, subtract your current age from that number.

Now you have a ballpark figure for how many years you've got left on the planet.

The question is: What are you going to do with them?

You can continue living in the past, beating yourself up about the money mistakes you made when you were younger, telling yourself you've left it too late…or you can rise up and make yourself proud.

Here's you: The economy sucks.

Here's me: More millionaires were created in the Great Depression than at any other time. Author and physician Peter Diamandis found that in the past century the average lifespan has doubled, while the average income has tripled. Food is 10 times cheaper, electricity is 20 times cheaper, transport is 100 times cheaper and communication is 1000 times cheaper. *These are* the good old days.

Stop with the excuses

These are all excuses. Every single one of them.

You can live the rest of your life with excuses about your lot—most people do—but they sure as hell won't protect you from the financial fire that's eventually going to work its way to you.

There are people who've sat where you are right now—with their self-confidence shot and with very little money or prospects—and they have singlehandedly clawed back control over their money and their life.

And you're going to meet some of them.

In this book, I'm going to introduce you to:

- a working-class couple who were convinced they'd left it too late…and are now on track to retire with a million-dollar nest egg

- a young man who doubled his money…and built his legacy

- a young woman who clawed her way out from under tens of thousands of dollars in credit card debt…and then helped her mother do the same

- a grief-stricken widow who was left in dire straits…who went on to put all her kids through private school

- a single woman who bought her (capital city, non-dogbox) home all on her very own…no man was part of her financial plan

- a mother whose husband's parting words were, 'You'll never survive financially without me'…who proved the jerk wrong.

They're people like you—just without the excuses.

The truth hurts, right?

It's kind of like when you see a picture of yourself on Facebook and think, 'Who's that fat bastard?'

When you're a bit flabby, there's no denying it. You know it. Your kids know it. You can't hide it. It's there on display for everybody to see and judge.

But it's the opposite when it comes to money. It's easy to hide your *financial* flab from the world.

I've found that it's often the most financially flabby people who appear to look the fittest. They can have a McMortgaged McMansion, a leased Lexus and a maxed-out platinum credit card, and you'd never know that behind closed doors they're the financial equivalent of pudgy North Korean dictator Kim Jong-un.

No-one knows that they're walking around with the financial equivalent of cankles.

At least if you've got a muffin top you've got the motivation to buy an Ab King Pro on a late-night infomercial, or sign up for Light n' Easy.

But if you *look* like you have a financial sixpack, you've got *zero* motivation to change. And that's why most people never do.

Facing up to the fact that you're not as successful or sorted as you tell yourself you are—or as your family and friends believe you to be—takes guts. It's like standing butt-naked in front of the mirror and looking at your gut. Stripped of your clothes, and excuses, there's no-one to blame but yourself for the situation you're in. You made your decisions. You decided to let yourself cruise.

That's the alpaca kick right there: seeing your situation for what it really is and having the courage to change it.

Success isn't found in the eyes of others: buying things you don't need, with money you don't have, to impress people you won't know in 20 years' time.

True and lasting success is knowing deep in your bones that you have the freedom to tread your own path in life, and the ability to protect those you love.

Be financially fireproof

Look, life is busy. Life is a messy bathroom, running late to your kids' footy matches, unpaid overtime, and collapsing at the end of the week on the couch with Indian takeaway and pappadum crumbs on your shirt.

If you try to do a million things, you'll do none.

Yet that's the power of focusing on just one thing—one step—and ticking it off the list.

Let me explain why this works with one last fire analogy.

Our fire plan was simple: on extreme risk days, Liz would pack up our son, leave the farm and head for the city. And on the morning of our fire, I was sitting at my kitchen table at the house, with my CFA-issued volunteer pager next to me.

It hadn't gone off … yet.

However, the smoke was starting to surround me, so I decided to drive to my neighbours', who live on a ridge, to get a better view of what the hell was going on.

I rounded up the dogs and put them in the back of the old farm ute, turned on the tranny, and got halfway down the driveway when the ABC Radio announcer said of my area, *It is too late to leave. You must take shelter now to protect yourself.*

Bugger.

When you're in the thick of a bushfire, it's too late to start thinking about what to do. You just need to be executing your plan like a patriotic North Korean soldier.

Here's how the CFA explains it:

> *A Bushfire Can Be a Terrifying Situation*
>
> *Strong gusty winds, intense heat and flames will make you tired quickly. Thick heavy smoke will sting your eyes and choke your lungs. It will be difficult to see and breathe.*
>
> *The roaring sound of the fire approaching could be frightening. Embers will rain down, causing spot fires around you. Power and water may be cut off. You may be isolated, and it will be dark, noisy and extremely demanding both mentally and physically.*
>
> *This is not the time to be making major decisions.*
>
> *Preparing your fire plan allows you to make major decisions in advance, and will help keep you focused and make better decisions in the event of a threat.*

And you know what?

The same rules apply when it comes to facing your financial fire: when you lose your job, or lose your partner or retire—it's *too late* to be making major decisions.

This book will make you financially fireproof—you will be *totally* prepared. You'll have made your major decisions in advance. You'll have everything on autopilot. You won't need to panic. You won't second-guess yourself. You'll know exactly what to do.

And the result is that you'll be able to say, 'I've got this'.

The secret is...

At this point, after all the talk of alpacas, sheep and farms, you may be forgiven for thinking you've picked up a country and western novel. My editor had similar concerns: 'Scott, I'd like to see more sunshine and positivity... and less fire, devastation and dead animals'.

Okay, so this is not your typical finance book.

Hell knows my publisher would have liked me to be a bit more 'self-helpy'. You see, one of the bestselling books of the past decade was *The Secret*. The guts of its message was that to achieve success all you need to do is picture something in your mind, and you'll achieve it.

Well, let's all get out a guitar, sit in a circle, hold hands and start strumming.

This book—and the solid-as-a-rock steps it gives you—is built on values that have stood the test of time. I learned a lot about life and money from my grandparents—they were part of the so-called Silent Generation who lived (and thrived) through the not-so-Great Depression.

What did that mean in a practical sense?

Well, they paid their bills on time... with cash.

They saved their money... rather than relying on credit cards.

They didn't expect handouts... being on the dole was something to be ashamed of.

They lived in modest homes—not McMansions—and they celebrated when they paid them off.

And they created a real legacy, which—ultimately—is what this book is all about.

Introducing the Barefoot Steps

Some finance books are wishy-washy on what you should do. They say things like, 'Write down your dreams'.

Others are written by weirdos who have colour-coded spreadsheets for their undies drawer and whose idea of a holiday is the Bendigo caravan park (communal toilet option). They give you a laundry list of things you *should* be doing, culminating with:

'You need to follow a strict written budget every single day.'

The truth?

I've never been able to stick to something as rigid as a budget, and I don't expect you to either.

For most people, budgets don't work. They're like surviving on a grapefruit diet.

Budgets set you up to fail. You feel like a loser with no willpower.

You're not. You are normal.

Here's the deal: the Barefoot Steps are *not* a cute way to organise a book.

They are nine specific steps that you complete in order, one by one.

The power of the Barefoot Steps is that they focus on you doing just *one thing* at a time.

You won't get overwhelmed.

You and I are going to plant your wealth tree, and get it growing.

THE BAREFOOT STEPS
ON ONE PAGE

 STEP 1
SCHEDULE A MONTHLY
BAREFOOT DATE NIGHT

 STEP 2
SET UP YOUR
BUCKETS

 **STEP 3**
DOMINO YOUR
DEBTS

 STEP 4
BUY YOUR HOME

 **STEP 5**
INCREASE YOUR SUPER
TO 15 PER CENT

  **STEP 6**
BOOST YOUR MOJO
TO THREE MONTHS

STEP 7
GET THE BANKER
OFF YOUR BACK

 **STEP 8**
NAIL YOUR
RETIREMENT
NUMBER

 STEP 9
LEAVE A LEGACY

Part 1

PLANT

It's time to get your hands dirty.

By the time we've finished the 'Plant' part of this book, you'll have built your entire financial infrastructure, and as a result you'll be tens, or even hundreds, of thousands of dollars better off.

See, this book isn't for flicking—it's for doing (preferably while eating garlic bread and drinking wine, as you'll see in a moment).

I'm not going to throw a bunch of generic tips at you.

Instead, I'm going to be super specific about the first three Barefoot Steps that I want you to follow to *plant* the seeds of your future wealth.

And if you've just read this and thought to yourself, 'Dude, my seeds are already planted', well I've got a few surprises in store for you.

I'm going to:

- show you how I manage my money in around 10 minutes a week, including the exact accounts I use

- detail how you can live—and spend—like a multimillionaire, even on a below-average income

- explain why I shut down my self-managed super fund (SMSF) ... and introduce you to the cheapest super fund in the world

- give you a specific script that you can follow to get 'wholesale' deals on your insurance

- show you how to turn dumping your debts into a game you'll enjoy playing—and winning.

Plus we'll sketch out the only financial plan you'll ever need—a plan so simple that it fits on the back of a serviette.

Let's dig in.

STEP 1

SCHEDULE A MONTHLY BAREFOOT DATE NIGHT

You love going out and eating nice food, right? And you've never seen a $50 note you didn't like, right?

Well, we're going to combine the two and have a Barefoot Date Night—once a week for the next five weeks (to get you up and running with the Barefoot Steps), and then monthly thereafter.

Money talk is better with garlic bread and wine

Once a week, for the next five weeks, you and your partner are going to get dressed up, go out to dinner and put in place the Barefoot Steps—that is, actually do them: set up some accounts, and have the conversations while you munch on garlic bread and have a glass of wine.

What if I'm single?

Well, you're in luck.

First, you can find a friend or family member you respect, give them this book and work your way through the steps together. However, I totally understand that you may not feel comfortable spilling your financial guts to someone.

If so, it's you and me, babe (or...dude).

I have permission from my wife for you to take me out (well, my book) and sort your money.

And you don't even have to do it at a restaurant. It could be a coffee shop or it could be your bedroom, though it's much more fun to make a date of it. The important thing is that you intentionally carve out time one night a week for the next five weeks (and then monthly, forever).

There are three reasons you should stop what you're doing and schedule your first Barefoot Date Night immediately:

- *First*, **because it'll make you happier.**

  The only thing that psychologists are unanimous on is that spending time with your family and friends is a direct predictor of wellbeing—and hands down one of the best things you can do for your relationship.

  Liz and I do our Barefoot Date Night on the first Tuesday of the month (the same day that the Reserve Bank meets to decide on interest rates ... how hot is that?). She gets dressed up, I comb my hair, and we go out for dinner and talk about our money.

  And let me tell you, it's a lot of fun.

  It's like kicking off tight shoes at the end of the day. The stresses and strains of life that buzz around your brain—work, the dishes, Facebook, the phone, the kids—fall away as you treat yourself for a few hours.

  You'll look forward to it, I promise.

  (And fellas, spending an evening with your partner talking about how committed you are to providing for your family—well, that's some good financial foreplay right there ... *mmm-hhmm, you know what I'm talk'n 'bout*.)

- *Second*, **because it's the two of you against the world.**

  That's the way I look at our marriage. Yes, we're parents, uncles and aunties, friends and bosses, but at our core we're just two big kids doing our best to create a life for our kids that makes us proud.

  And if you're going to create an amazing life that isn't dictated by financial fears, you've got to work together and back each other up. There's no time for indecision—you're fighting for your family.

  There's no way around it: you need your partner on board. And years of experience has taught me that the way to get them on board is with nice food, a sprinkling of booze and a copy of my book.

And if you're single, the good news is you don't have to play the partner mind games. You only have to look after yourself. This is going to be a snap.

- **Third, because there's no such thing as 'get rich quick'.**

  Most people can get themselves financially sorted in one year, then go on to become financially successful in six years. Yes, those are rubbery figures. A guesstimate. But after helping thousands of people over many years, I've found them to be pretty much bang on.

In Step 4 you'll meet Danielle, a single woman from Melbourne in her early 30s. Six years ago she was on the bones of her backside, working in admin, with credit card debts. Today she owns her own home and has emergency savings and a share portfolio. Even better, she did it all on her own: no boyfriend, no rich parents—just my plan and *grit*.

Here's another thought: stop for a second and work out where you were six years ago.

Go on … do it.

It seems like yesterday, right? It's likely the next six will too.

But if you don't make a commitment to starting today, nothing will change.

The good news is that you can do astonishing things in six years, but only if you schedule your Barefoot Date Nights right now.

Yep, this is where my apple tree analogy comes in …

Plant the bloody tree now!

Your future self will thank you for it.

Truth is, most people totally *over*estimate what they can achieve in one year, but totally *under*estimate what they can do in six years.

So to reiterate: you're going to schedule five weekly Barefoot Date Nights—after which it's monthly, forever.

I don't care if you're in your 20s or your 70s, whether you're gay, straight, married or single. Making a ritual of focusing on your money is the most powerful thing you can do. Period.

Schedule your first five Barefoot Date Nights

Please pull out your phone, or go to your diary (or Facebook, or kitchen calendar, or whatever you use to track your schedule) and book in your Barefoot Date Night each week for the next five weeks.

I promise it will be worth it...

In just five 'date nights' you and I are going to radically change your financial life.

(With a drink in your hand.)

Barefoot Date Night confessions

April Mac, NSW

I have never felt so financially secure as I am now … I feel excited about my future.

I was never under any great financial difficulty—I just never really had any money. I always had a job and earned enough to get by, but I spent everything I made each week.

My biggest problem was not thinking long term about my finances. I honestly just didn't think my husband and I could ever earn enough to be wealthy.

My sister got me onto Barefoot on the 1st of January 2014. I signed up in the middle of the night and read through everything I could. I was so excited to have a New Year's resolution that didn't involve dieting! I started by setting some simple goals to achieve by the 1st of January 2015.

Well, in 12 months I achieved everything I set out to achieve. And I did it all while earning half my regular salary, as I was on maternity leave.

Not only that—since joining Barefoot, I've managed to:

- pay $30 000 off our mortgage
- save another $30 000 for renovating our home
- take the family to Fiji, Hamilton Island and Noosa
- build a share portfolio worth $16 000
- save up a nice little emergency money account ('Mojo') …

… all while not having to sacrifice my lifestyle (I am ashamed to say I eat breakfast out more than I do at home).

Barefoot helped me visualise the bigger picture. I could see myself in the success stories of others, and it made me determined to be the one to provide financial security for my family (not Oz Lotto).

The only problem is, I never shut up about Barefoot and everyone is sick of me mentioning it. But I will continue to try and convince everyone because I've seen how far it has taken me in two short years. I know I am nothing special, so I think it can work for anyone.

I have never felt as financially secure as I am now, even when I was earning twice as much and didn't have a child to take care of. I feel excited about my future.

Barefoot banking

Given this is our first Barefoot Date Night, I want you to go out for dinner and really treat yourself.

I'm serious.

Get ready to buy the best thing on the menu and have a nice glass of wine (or two).

Why?

Because, with about half an hour's work, you're going to save yourself $477 over the next year—and thousands of dollars over the next decade—by banishing bank fees from your life forever.

That's right, you'll never have to worry about sticking your card in a so-called *foreign* ATM and getting the banking equivalent of herpes (the dreaded $2 'FU fee').

What you're going to do is set up the accounts that will form the backbone of the Barefoot Steps, allowing you to automate your day-to-day finances to the point that you'll be able to manage your money in around 10 minutes a week.

Literally, while you're having your 'wine time', you're going to set up your new zero-fee accounts via the wonder of the mobile phone.

Most people never get around to doing this. Instead, they flick through a finance book and put it back on the shelf—but not you. Never underestimate yourself with a drink in your hand.

Of course, this will mean making some changes to your current banking arrangements.

> **Here's you:** Ugh! You want me to change my bank accounts? I really…can't be bothered.

> **Here's me:** Your current bank account is a lot like your last boyfriend. You knew he was a bit of a dud, that he was draining you and that he was never going to change. Your current bank account is also draining you: the average Australian household gets whacked with $477 in bank fees each year (according to the Reserve Bank). Over 10 years that's $4770—enough to take you to New York City and stay at a five-star hotel.

> **Here's you:** Yeah, but I have all my direct debits set up. It would be such a pain…

> **Here's me:** The real pain comes from dealing with a bank that slugs you with all sorts of annoying fees, and having to think about it (even if it's for a fraction of a second when you're using a foreign ATM and that smug little comment comes up: 'You will be charged $2 for this transaction—press to continue').

Plus, switching isn't a big deal. If you call your bank they'll give you a list of all your direct debits over the past 13 months. And your new bank should bend over backwards (or at least limbo a little) to get your business. Often they'll have templates and other hacks that you can email to your existing billers.

Anyway, I think of it like this: having an awesome bank account is a self-confidence thing. It's the little wins—the habits you build—that strengthen your confidence.

Or think of it like surfing: sure, you have to paddle a bit at the start (with a freaking wine in your hand), but once you catch that wave, you can relax and let it carry you home.

How did you get your current bank account?

Maybe it was your parents' bank.

Maybe it was bundled with your home loan (they probably called it a 'package').

Maybe you were a Dollarmite (more on this in Step 3).

If you're dealing with one of the Big Four banks, there's every chance you're getting screwed. Earning zero per cent interest is like sooo noughties.

So let's get into it.

Now, I'm not just going to waffle on about generic accounts—we're in this together, so I'm also going to show you *exactly* the accounts I use myself.

I'm going to take you through them one by one, and at the end I'll put it all together for you in a simple 'menu' for you to follow when you go on your first Barefoot Date Night.

Banishing bank fees from your life forever

'What do you look for in your banking relationship?' a bank executive once asked me.

'I'm sorry, but I'm just not looking for a relationship with a bank right now,' I told him, and then added, 'it's not me, it's you'.

I am *not* loyal to any financial institution.

Banks are giant corporate octopuses with tentacles that wrap around you and squeeze out as much money as they can.

According to the Australia Institute, we get charged the highest bank fees in the world. As I've said, the average Australian household gets whacked $477 a year. Makes sense when you think about it—how else could four businesses make $30 billion a year in profits in a country with just 24 million people?

Rant over.

The bottom line is that it doesn't pay to be loyal.

What you need from your bank is a dead-simple, zero-fee solution.

Spare me all the convoluted 'Terms & Conditions' and fine print: 'If you deposit $125 a month and don't withdraw it for 3 years, we'll pay you a bonus 0.16 per cent for the first 2 months, at which time it will revert back to our standard variable rate'.

Huh?

Just give me zero fees. As in doughnuts. None. Ever.*

(*And that includes no ATM fees. Ever.)

I don't care if I'm at one of those weirdly named convenience stores that has one of those weirdly named ATMs charging you an arm and half a leg to get your dough. Not my problem. I'm not paying for it.

Contrast this to a friend of mine who banks with ANZ. I spent 30 minutes with him one night trudging around the city in the rain looking for his ATM: 'I swear it was on the corner of Collins and Swanston!' he moaned while I stood there shivering, hating him.

My zero-fee everyday transaction account

If you stole my wallet, here's what you'd find:

A picture of me and my golden retriever, Buffett, frolicking on the grass, and...

My ING Orange Everyday debit card.

This is a corker of an account. (And remember: I get paid nothing for this recommendation. I'm fiercely independent and have no tie-ups with any financial institution, whatsoever.)

In fact, I like the account so much I want you to set up two of them.

And I want you to give them nicknames (this is easy to do with online banking—just ask your bank if you're not sure how it works).

Call one 'Daily Expenses' and the other 'Splurge'. Trust me on this—exactly *why* I'm asking you to give them these nicknames will be revealed in Step 2.

The reason I chose the ING Orange Everyday account is because it has zero fees. As in none. Not even those foreign ATM fees. (And that adds up. According to RateCity, 'two in every five ATM transactions are made at a machine not owned by the customer's bank network'.)

The downside? Well, into one of the accounts (make it 'Daily Expenses') you need to deposit $1000 every month (your wage, for example, which is easy).

Steal my wife's purse

Now if you stole my wife's purse...she'd be very upset.

And you'd find an ING Orange Everyday debit card, just like mine (and a lovely picture of our family—no dogs).

See, one of our iron-clad rules is that we keep the same account.

No, not like cute matching cards so that we're colour coordinated. And no, not just one card between us. (That would be weird: 'Honey, I'm just popping down the shops. Can I have *the* card?')

What I mean is that we have separate cards for the same bank accounts.

And, most importantly, we have an agreement that we can each spend up to $400 on whatever we choose. No need to ask for permission. Anything over that we talk about, and make a joint decision.

(And that's a good thing. Personally, I am deeply offended by how much her hairdresser charges. My barber hasn't changed his '$20 short back and sides' pricing in 15 years. Though, admittedly, she looks a *lot* better than I do.)

It's my firm belief that if you're married you should be sharing the same bank account, and all your finances.

Get some interest, brah!

You need to earn a decent interest rate on your savings. Granted, when interest rates are low, earning enough interest each year to buy a soap on a rope is almost *mission impossible*.

Yet that doesn't mean you should keep all your dough in your everyday transaction account, which pays 'two parts of bugger-all' (that is actually a finance term) in interest.

 What you want is separate online saver accounts that are linked to your everyday transaction account.

 In addition, you want the ability to move your money when needed and to set up automated triggers (we'll get to that later in Step 2, where we'll put your money on autopilot so you don't have to continually make decisions).

My linked high-interest online savings accounts

For high-interest online savings accounts I use ING Savings Maximisers that are linked to my ING Orange Everyday account. The ING Savings Maximisers consistently offer some of the highest interest on the market.

I want you to set up two of them—and again I want you to give them nicknames. Call one 'Smile' and the other 'Fire Extinguisher'.

(WTF, Barefoot! These names are getting crazier by the minute! Trust me on this and I'll explain all in Step 2.)

Here's a screenshot of my set-up.

By the way, with these online saver accounts I am not a 'rate tart'. I have no interest in switching accounts every time some other institution offers a piddly 0.15 per cent extra interest. It's just not worth my time. In summary: Zero fees. Good interest. All in one account. Simple.

(You may have more time on your hands, perhaps because you live at home with your mum and she does your ironing and plaits your hair, leaving you free to pore over spreadsheets on a Saturday night. If that's you, feel free to look at ME Bank, which at the time of writing is paying a bee's dick—another finance term—more interest than the ING Savings Maximiser.)

In any event you'll notice that I deal exclusively with online banks for these accounts. There's a reason for this: they do better deals because they've got lower overheads.

Plus, they're fighting against the Big Four, who rely on a mixture of apathy and a reputation for safety (which is rubbish, because the government guarantees all deposits—up to $250 000 per financial institution—for all local and international authorised deposit-taking institutions).

Get some Mojo, baby

Finally, you should have one bank account completely separate from your day-to-day banking.

I'm talking another *financial institution* altogether.

Why?

Because I want to make it hard-ish to get at this money.

This account will become what I call your 'Mojo'.

The aim of the Mojo account is to get your Mojo back, baby. So you don't have to stress about money like everyone else.

So what is it?

Well, it's not a redraw facility. It's not shares.

It's cold, hard cash in the bank.

And it's hard to access. You see, managing your money is about behaviour.

Most people shuffle money around from one account to another without ever actually saving any of it.

Now, the number one question people ask me about Mojo is this:

'Barefoot, can't I use my offset account for my Mojo?'

My answer?

It's not how I did it, but sure, you can if you want. The most important thing is that you do it!

My Mojo account

My Mojo account is a UBank USaver (UBank is NAB's 'Jetstar' brand).

No prizes for guessing the nickname this time: 'Mojo'.

As I've said, I deliberately keep it separate from my day-to-day banking because I don't want to be tempted to spend it. It's for emergencies like, say, your house burning down. And it's a good feeling knowing that you have a separate pot of money that can be your 'get out of jail free' card when you need it.

And if you have a mortgage...

When I had a mortgage, I was given a 'professional package' by the bank, which included a credit card (I chopped it up) and a basic bank account.

If you have a home loan, you've probably got a professional package too. Everyone gets one. It's a marketing gimmick designed to flog you as many high-cost products as possible.

I tried to screw down the same deal with my home loan provider as ING's zero-fee banking (especially the zero ATM fees). They just laughed at me. So I made ING Orange Everyday my 'Money HQ' and organised a direct debit to my home loan.

Simple.

Right, I've mentioned a few accounts so far, but maybe it's not quite clear in your mind. So I'm going to put it all together on a 'menu' for your Barefoot Date Night...

Note to future readers

If you've just picked up this book and it's 2027, perhaps ING and UBank aren't around anymore. It doesn't matter—the same rules apply: no fees. Ever. Always use internet banking (or whatever it is you call the internet now). And always get high rates of interest on your savings.

BAREFOOT DATE NIGHT MENU

Week 1

Choose somewhere really fancy for your very first Barefoot Date Night.

Trust me, you can afford to splurge—you're about to save yourself thousands of dollars in just 10 minutes.

ENTREE:

Whip out your phone and apply for:

- 2 × everyday transaction accounts—call them 'Daily Expenses' and 'Splurge' and get an ATM card for each (it's easier if you get your 'Daily Expenses' card first, then simply open another account for 'Splurge')
- 2 × online savings accounts—call them 'Smile' and 'Fire Extinguisher' and link them both to 'Daily Expenses'.

The entire process takes 10 minutes and can be done on your phone between entree and main course.

MAIN COURSE:

Next, I want you to apply online for:

- 1 × online savings account with a different institution—call it 'Mojo'.

When you open your separate Mojo account, I'd like you to *set it up with an initial $2000 deposit*. And if you don't have a spare $2000, look around your house and see what you can flog on Gumtree.

I'm dead serious.

Make it your mission to get $2000 in Mojo. It's a great kick-off for what will become the most psychologically important account you ever create. When you have Mojo, you don't have financial emergencies.

DESSERT:

It's time to get on the fizz. Have yourself some champagne (glass, or bottle).

You've earned it: it's not every day you save yourself from paying off some wanker banker's BMW.

And it's only getting better. On next week's Barefoot Date Night, I'm going to show you how to make up to $226 484 by screwing down an amazing deal on your super.

The world's cheapest super fund

Last week (well, last Barefoot Date Night), you brought a couple of brand-spanking-new everyday transaction accounts into the world, opened a bunch of high-interest online savings accounts and stopped getting slugged with bank fees.

Nice one!

This week it's time to make some serious, life-changing cashola.

I'm talking potentially hundreds of thousands of dollars, in as little as one hour.

And I'm going to show you exactly how to do it.

In fact, I'll show you exactly how *I* do it.

'I've got this'

The Barefoot Steps will prepare you to look life in the eye and say … 'I've got this'.

You've now got $2000 in Mojo (or at least I hope you have).

That will help eliminate your *short-term* money dramas.

This week is all about eliminating your *long-term* money worries. And the vehicle for doing this (whether you're 19 or 90) is superannuation.

What you do in the next hour is going to have a direct and amazing impact on the 8670 evenings you'll spend in retirement (okay, it's an average, but you get the point—it's a long time).

Simply put, you will have more money. In fact, depending on your current situation, you could have over $1 *million more* if you follow the Barefoot Steps.

Here's the point: I've sat knee to knee with scared and frail retirees who are too worried about their money to turn on a heater. The biggest difference this hour will make is that you won't have to worry about money when you're old.

And if you're in your 50s, 60s or 70s, what I'm going to walk you through is even more important than for the young-uns. The dirty secret of the finance industry is that you'll pay two-thirds of your super fees *after* you retire—when you can least afford to.

Now, on last week's Barefoot Date Night I told you that you should treat yourself with the money you'll save on bank fees.

Tonight?

You can buy the entire freaking restaurant with all the money you're going to save.

Actually, I'm joking. Do not do this. (Restaurants are terrible investments, which is why good chefs are forced to go on reality cooking shows to earn their money.)

This is the finance geek's version of UFC—it's bare-knuckle financial fighting. And with me as your coach, you're going to win.

Don't skim this: I mean, when was the last time you made $226 484 in an hour!?

Ding, ding, let's jump in the ring.

The greatest tax dodge in Australia

Let me count the ways I love super:

First: for all the trash that's talked about super, it's still hands-down the greatest tax dodge going round. It's even better than a Cayman Islands bank account, because the average worker can *legally* use super to cut their tax. While the top tax rate for individuals is 47 per cent (including the Medicare levy), you'll pay just 15 per cent on the money that goes into your super fund.

Second: you can retire with $1.6 million in super and you won't pay a cent of tax. (And as long as ageing Baby Boomers keep voting with their feet, this is unlikely to change.)

Third: your super is protected if you go bankrupt.

And yet most people treat their super like the shirtless stoner trying to wash their windshield at the traffic lights (Do. Not. Look).

> **Here's you:** I don't really pay much attention to my super.

> **Here's me:** Oh yes you do. In fact, last month you spent around 15 hours on it. It's called the 'Super Guarantee'—compulsory superannuation, in other words.

Basically, the government doesn't trust you to save for your retirement, so they order your boss to skim 9.5 per cent off your wage (which is how I got the 15-hours-a-month figure) and put it into a super fund.

Yet the overwhelming majority of people don't spend even 15 minutes choosing which super fund they want for their precious money. Instead, they just join the fund they're offered when they get the job. Worse, the average Aussie has four super funds from different employers, each one getting whacked with fees.

And that's exactly how the super industry likes it.

Middle-aged men ruin everything

As a general rule, finance guys cock everything up.

And, as a general rule, finance guys are white, balding and middle-aged.

When it comes to super, they've taken a beautiful thing and corrupted it.

And *another* bunch of (mostly) white, balding men—our nation's politicians—haven't exactly covered themselves in glory either. Our $2.6 trillion of savings is like a honeypot for them. They just can't help but tinker with the rules.

Back to the finance guys: this industry skims $31 billion each year from our super funds. And we have some of the highest investment management fees in the world, according to the OECD, which tracks these things.

Mark my words—many boats, mansions, planes and overseas junkets have been bought from compulsory superannuation. From *your* nest egg.

The upshot is, when it comes to super, most people get robbed—with a pen.

Let me introduce you to one such person.

The gold-plated urinal

Each week for over a decade, I've been answering readers' financial questions in the newspaper. Yet, of the thousands of questions, there's only one response I've written that's given my editor serious heart palpitations. Here's the question I received:

Dear Barefoot,

I'm getting close to retirement, and hence I'm really starting to think about my super (better late than never!). I opened a fund with AMP back in 1991 and it's built up to $330 000. I am paying 1.5 per cent per annum in fees, and also 'recovery and administration' costs of 0.5 per cent, though I can't make head or tail of what these are. What would you suggest?

Frank

Frank thought he'd done the right thing.

After all, his super was with AMP, one of Australia's largest, oldest and most trusted financial institutions (well, until the Royal Commission anyway). And he'd diligently invested his money over 25 years.

And yet, by my calculations, Frank had paid AMP roughly $85 000 in fees over that period. That's a lot of money—a little over a quarter of his life savings!

I answered Frank's question as follows:

Dear Frank,

I suggest you call AMP. Perhaps you might suggest they honour your contribution by way of a gold-plated plaque at AMP HQ. They could mount it in the toilets and it'd say, 'This urinal was paid for by Frank from Bendigo's super fund over a 25-year period'.

Barefoot

My editor almost had a heart attack (but he chose to publish it anyway).

AMP was very angry.

Yet no-one thought much about poor old Frank, who was the one who really deserved to be pissed off.

Your super fund can gobble up a third of your savings in fees

Guess what?

You could be Frank.

Your super could be paying off some fund manager's Ferrari.

Research by Rainmaker shows that a person who starts work at 20 could accumulate up to $663 000 in super over their working life. However, they will also pay $174 000 in fees, on average.

If there's one thing you take from this book, make it this:

Choosing an ultra-low-cost super fund is the easiest way to win a game that millions of people lose.

And in a moment I'm going to show you how to choose one.

But right now we need to talk about how you're getting screwed.

The $226 484 difference

Let's say a 35-year-old has $50 000 in a fund and contributes $5000 a year over the next 30 years with an investment return rate of 8 per cent. The difference between investing in a fund that charges 1 per cent a year in fees and one that charges 0.02 per cent a year is a whopping $226 484, according to the 2016 ASIC MoneySmart Managed Fund Fees Calculator. In this graph, 'your fund' is the higher fee one, and the 'alternative fund' is the lower fee one.

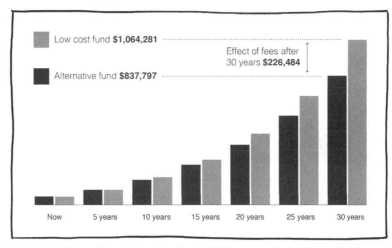

Source: ASIC MoneySmart Managed Fund Fees Calculator. This is not a typical managed fund scenario and should be used for the purpose of comparing the impact of fees in a hypothetical situation only.

What about fancy investment options?

You don't need to worry about an extensive range of individual investment options within your super.

(In Step 5, we'll discuss everything you need to know about investing, but for now we're just focusing on the things you can control, like the fees you pay.)

Think of these fancy options as the Spaghetti Meatball Pizza on the menu at your local chew-and-spew. Sure, it sounds interesting, but you know you're just going to order the same Hawaiian you've ordered for the past 15 years.

If that's you, relax—you're normal. There's a scientific term for this behaviour: the paradox of choice. Faced with too many options, the average person will be inclined to choose none.

Exhibit A of the paradox of choice?

Approximately 90 per cent of the Australian population don't choose where their super money is invested, so they end up in their fund's default option. This is a 'balanced' fund that balances your money across a mix of assets—generally seven parts shares and three parts cash and fixed interest.

Note

Before you do anything, it's important to talk to an independent, fee-for-service financial advisor. There are tax and insurance issues you need to be on top of before you make any switch. (I'll show you how to find a good financial advisor in Step 8.)

People who simply accept this option aren't even choosing the Hawaiian.

Hell, they don't even know where the pizza shop is.

They're just sitting at their dining-room table, staring at the wall, with their mouths open.

Here's the thing: not all default funds are created equal. That's why you need to check where your money is actually invested.

So, how do you find an ultra-low-cost super fund? I'll show you real soon (when I put it all together in the menu for Barefoot Date Night Week 2).

All the questions you've been too bored to ask about your super— in one-and-a-bit pages

Should I open a self-managed super fund (SMSF)?

Probably not.

Ask anyone who runs their own SMSF and they'll tell you it's a pain in the rump. That's because the government makes you jump through the same compliance hoops that billion-dollar funds have to.

However, they do make excellent investment vehicles for Old Stubby Fingers, your accountant, who'll lock you into paying over a grand a year for auditing and compliance. Basically, unless you're a small-business owner wanting to buy your work premises in your super fund, I wouldn't bother.

I did the research and, when I looked at it logically, I shut down my own SMSF.

Can I choose a new super fund?

Most people can. However, some people who are covered by industrial agreements, or are members of defined benefit funds, can't. Ask your payroll officer.

What investment option should I choose for my super?

If you haven't made a choice it will be in a default 'balanced' fund, which, as the name implies, balances your money across a mix of assets—generally seven parts shares and three parts cash and fixed interest (or thereabouts). That's not a bad option to start with. But if you're under 45, invest in the 'growth' option.

How can I be certain my boss is putting money into my super fund?

Good question. Don't believe your payslip. Call your fund and check that the money has been paid.

How do I find my lost super?

If you've got your super in multiple funds, roll them into the one to avoid getting whacked with extra fees. You can do this through your ATO account on myGov (my.gov.au) where you can also find your lost super.

Should I be making extra contributions to my super?

Yes, but only after you buy your family home. Don't get too stressed about this right now—just keep reading and I'll lay it all out in good time (in Step 5, actually).

When can I access my super?

Generally between the ages of 55 and 60, if you retire or start a 'transition to retirement' pension. Otherwise, you can access it when you're 65 regardless of whether you're still working or not.

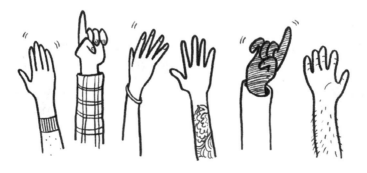

The super fund I use

My wife and I used to have a self-managed super fund (SMSF)...because that's what wealthy, sophisticated people do, right?

Two things made me shut it down:

First: I wanted simplicity. I love investing (that's why I'm the Barefoot Investor). But Liz? Not so much. And given that she's younger than me, and fitter than me, the chances are she'll outlive me. And an SMSF would be a technical and administrative nightmare for her.

Second: I found the lowest cost fund in the world.

The super fund I invest in is hands down the lowest cost super fund in the country. In fact, I believe it's the lowest cost fund in the world.

And guess what?

It's also beaten the average return by super funds over both five and seven years.

It's the Hostplus Indexed Balanced Fund, and it charges a tiny investment management fee of 0.06 per cent. In other words, 6 cents for every $100 invested (plus a $78 a year admin fee).

And, just to be clear, this is a plain Jane index-tracking fund: it automatically buys shares in the biggest 200 companies in Australia (think the banks, BHP, Woolies, Wesfarmers). And it automatically buys the 1500 biggest companies in the United States, Europe, Japan and elsewhere (think Apple, Facebook, Nestlé). And it automatically invests the rest in high-interest cash and fixed interest accounts.

Sounds boring, right?

You bet it is.

Yet this boring fund has beaten the pants off most stock-pickers.

The truth is, most managers don't beat the market over the long term. That's because to get market-beating returns they've got to jump a big hurdle first: their fees.

The higher the fees they charge, the bigger the return needed just to keep pace with Mr Average. Research from Standard & Poor's shows that over a five-year term just 10 per cent of Australian fund managers beat the market. The rest fell short. So a fund with dirt-cheap running costs gets a huge head start.

BAREFOOT DATE NIGHT MENU

Week 2

Fund managers like to eat at expensive restaurants and drink expensive wine…and then charge it to their expense account. Guess who ultimately picks up the tab? Hard-working super members. It's kind of like the opposite of sponsoring an African kid: 'part of your fees helps us feed our (pasty white, tubby, pinstriped-suit-wearing) executive his lobster and wild prawn medley'.

ENTREE:

The aim of this Barefoot Date Night is for you to invest in a super fund that charges ultra-low fees. However, you probably have no idea what you're currently being charged.

So I want you to take out your phone and google the following:

'[The name of your fund] + PDS'.

This search will bring up a PDF of the PDS (welcome to the wonderful world of acronyms!). PDS stands for 'product disclosure statement', and almost no-one ever reads it.

Next, scroll down to the 'Fees and charges' section.

Your super fund should be charging you less than 0.85 per cent a year in fees—total. If it's higher than that, you should seriously think about switching to a cheaper fund.

MAIN COURSE:

Depending on how your 'Fees and charges' search went, you may have a bit of indigestion.

If so, you can apply on your phone for a new, ultra-low-cost fund in around 10 minutes—though going through the steps of rolling over your accounts and making sure your insurance is sorted will take a little longer. Still, it's hard to understate just how much of an impact this will have on your future.

DESSERT:

This is no time for counting calories: order something rich and thick (like Donald Trump).

Well, that's Barefoot Date Night Week 2 done—and your super sorted. In the next Barefoot Date Night we're going to tackle something that's crucial to your safety and that of your family. Something no-one wants to talk about...so you and I are going talk about it.

Starting over in your 50s

Matt Ledger, WA

The name Barefoot stuck in my memory, so I googled it and my life began to gain some direction.

Divorce left me financially destitute.

At age 54 and with only a few crumbs left in savings, I continued to put my daughter through her final two years of school while supporting both her and my son. As you'd expect, this drained all the savings I had left after the split.

All of a sudden it became apparent that I was running out of time. At 54, with no home, no savings and virtually no super, the picture was grim.

I approached financial advisors, brokers, bank managers and financial planners, all of whom pretty much laughed at my situation (more to the point, they saw no money in it for them). It was difficult to see a way forward. I really did think that life sucked.

I then overheard a couple talking about investments and the name 'Barefoot' stuck in my memory, so I googled it and started reading everything I could find that Scott had written—and my life began to gain some direction.

My first step was to change careers, as I realised I wasn't going to get anywhere working in real estate, with inconsistent income.

So I sent off 237 job applications—and got two responses.

At that point, I decided to re-endorse my heavy vehicle licence and went back to driving road trains in WA. As unglamorous as it may sound, it re-established me financially. And it's simply the most uplifting, liberating feeling one could ask for.

Having started around a year ago, I've now put away $5700 in savings, built up $15000 in my Mojo account and turned a very poor SMSF into something resembling a future to look forward to.

I have even rejoined the mortgage ranks (after being rejected many times) and have built a new home. It's small but nonetheless mine, and it's giving back some stability to my children, who've stayed with me for the duration.

In five years I hope to have $35000 in savings, $75000 in Mojo, and super ticking away towards $1 million.

My children, both young adults now, often comment on how much happier I am these days. My response is that my financial future now looks positive. Without daily money woes to contend with, a weight's been lifted off my shoulders.

And the coaching has begun—teaching my two kids to start on the journey to financial freedom, the Barefoot way!

For me, the mental and emotional recovery—and the resulting return of my self-confidence and self-belief—has been nothing short of profound.

This has given me new hope for my future.

Your insurance sorted in one beer

Welcome to the third Barefoot Date Night. This week is all about protecting your assets.

According to a reliable source (the English tabloids), Kim Kardashian has insured her arse for more than $US21 million.

For me, this raises a couple of questions:

Why does she even need insurance? After all, she's apparently worth $US175 million.

And why is she only insuring her arse? I mean, how do you even break your arse? (On second thoughts, I'm sure Kanye has rapped about it: 'My wife got a million dollar boo-tay'.)

Yes, while other guys spend their nights watching her home movies, I lie awake analysing her insurance exposure.

Welcome to the crazy world of insurance!

For our third Barefoot Date Night I'm going to show you how to protect yourself against the bad stuff that could happen.

And of course when it comes to insurance, I've got form.

See, the day our house burned down was the worst day of my family's life.

But it could have been a lot worse. According to CommBank, for every family like ours that loses its home in a fire, *four* families lose their home because of the death of a breadwinner, and 48 families lose their home because of a breadwinner becoming disabled.

Don't think it will happen to you?

Well, according to CommBank (again), two in five Australians will suffer a critical illness by the age of 65.

The bottom line is this: you can do all the right things, you can have everything sorted, and something you have no control over can wipe you out financially.

Trust me, it does happen. This is what I do for a living. I'm the guy the young father calls when he's been diagnosed with a terminal illness.

Yes, this is uncomfortable, but it's not about you—it's about the people you love.

Heavy, huh?

Can't we get back to the Kimmy butt gags?

Don't stress—I'm going to give you a solid, no-fuss plan to protect you and your loved ones. I've not only got your back, I've even got tried and tested word-for-word scripts for you to follow when dealing with the insurance heavyweights.

The golden rules of insurance

Rule 1: Only insure against things that can kill you financially

Your iPhone breaking will not kill you financially, so don't take out extended warranty insurance.

But you should insure against:

- your house burning down (been there) or getting robbed (been there too)
- your car getting into a bingle (multiple times)
- travelling overseas and getting sick (once)
- going to hospital (a couple of times)
- death or permanent disablement (never, touch wood)
- being unable to work (not so far).

Rule 2: Choose a higher excess

In the event of a claim, you can choose to pay an initial amount towards your costs, which is known as an 'excess'. The more excess you're prepared to cough up, the cheaper your annual insurance premium will be.

You now have Mojo, which means you can afford a higher excess. Do it.

Rule 3: Don't automatically pay your insurance premium each year

Insurance companies behave like douchebag cheating husbands. They sweet-talk new customers, showering them with discounts and gifts, while treating their faithful wives at home (that's you, the existing customer) like dirt. The easiest money you'll make is calling them each year and telling them you're thinking of switching.

Hang on, why are you still reading?

Why don't you have your phone in your hand already?

Okay, here's a word-for-word script that you'll use with your current insurers to lower your car, house and contents insurance:

> **You:** Hello, I'd like to increase my excess to $750 per claim. How much will that reduce my annual premium by?
>
> **Insurance rep:** One moment please.
>
> **You (googling 'best offer' + the name of your insurance company):** And I see you're offering a 15 per cent discount to new customers who join before the end of the month…
>
> **Insurance rep:** That's only for new customers, sir.
>
> **You:** Well, paint me red and call me Randy—I'm your newest customer!
>
> **Insurance rep:** I'll talk to my supervisor.
>
> **You:** I'll wait.

Insurance rep: Good news, sir. You can definitely save 25 per cent by increasing your excess. And, because you're such a valued customer, we've also been able to give you the discount that we normally only give to new customers.

You: Thank you! Now just make sure it's backdated from yesterday.

Now, let's talk about the two types of insurance that are probably screwing you over.

Private health insurance—do you even need it?

If you're under 31, you probably don't need private health insurance. And if you're earning under $90 000 as a single person, or under $180 000 as a family, you probably don't need it either.

That's because Australia has one of the best public health systems on the planet. If you get sick or have an accident, you'll get five-star treatment in a public hospital and lump it on the taxpayer.

However, if you're earning over $90 000 as a single or over $180 000 as a couple, you'll get hit with an extra tax (called the Medicare Levy Surcharge), which is equivalent to the cost of private health cover. So you may as well pay it and get the private health insurance!

Another reason to pay up is that if you want your family to go to the front of the queue and choose your own doctor, you'll need to go private.

Right, so if you do need it, here are my golden rules to getting better private health cover for less than you're paying right now:

- **Purchase top-level 'comprehensive' private hospital insurance.**

  I get the best hospital cover I can for my money.

- **Don't purchase extras or 'combined' healthcare cover.**

  If I want a Swedish massage, I'll pay for it out of my own pocket. Most of the 'extras' in insurance policies can cost you hundreds of bucks extra a year whether you claim or not. Don't believe me? Ring your fund and request an annual claim statement. Then ask, 'If I switched to a comparable "hospital only" policy, how much would I save each year?'

- **Stay away from iSelect.**

  iSelect is Australia's most-visited health insurance 'comparison site' (picture me doing the inverted commas with my fingers). But iSelect isn't a genuine comparison site at all. It's a sales page tarted up to look like a comparison site. Of the 35 health insurers operating in Australia, iSelect lets you pick from just 12. The big players, Bupa and Medibank Private for example, at the time of writing aren't on the list.

  Same goes for that crazy meerkat dude and all the rest. Instead, go to the government's search engine, PrivateHealth.gov.au, which lists *every* health provider.

Protecting your family

Your most powerful financial asset isn't your home or your car: it's your ability to earn an income.

If you have school-age kids and you don't have income protection insurance (also called income *replacement* insurance), you're normal: according to OnePath, 94 per cent of Aussie families don't have it.

AND THEY ARE COMPLETELY INSANE

Every day, 18 Australian families lose a working-age parent. Every year, 235790 working-age parents suffer a serious illness or injury and more than 17000 of them are forced to stop working, either permanently or for an extended time.

Thankfully, there's an easy fix, and it takes just one phone call.

So call your super fund.

Now, your fund will probably offer a (tax-deductible) *default* level of life cover (if you're dead), total permanent disability (if you're nearly dead) and income protection (if you're crook).

It's good...but not good enough.

So how much cover do you need?

A rule of thumb is 10 to 12 times your annual income, if you have young kids. And if you're a stay-at-home mum, you *can* and *should* get life cover and total permanent disability insurance as well, because if you weren't around all hell would break loose and your hubby would need to employ two people to cover all the work you do (childcare, cooking, cleaning, and so on).

Look, this is so important that I've written another script for you to use with your super fund:

> **You:** Hello, I'd like to talk to one of your qualified insurance experts about my level of cover for life, TPD and income protection.
>
> **Super fund customer service:** One moment, I'll transfer you.
>
> **Qualified insurance expert:** Can I help you?
>
> **You:** I'd like you to provide me with an insurance quote for 12 times my annual salary of combined life and TPD insurance. In addition, I'd also like you to provide me a quote on income protection for 75 per cent of my wage till I reach the age of 65. I'm happy to wait 90 days before I claim.
>
> **Qualified insurance expert:** Yes, I can do that.
>
> **You:** Also, I don't want my super contributions eaten up by the cost of paying for this insurance, so can you tell me how much more money I need to put into super to cover the cost of the extra insurance?
>
> **Qualified insurance expert:** Of course.
>
> **You:** Thanks. Can you put all this in writing and send it to me so I can look over it with my partner, just to make sure we're on the same page?

BAREFOOT DATE NIGHT MENU

Week 3

For this Barefoot Date Night you should go Mexican. (Do it for me. I wish I could—my wife doesn't like spicy food.) Tonight, it boils down to this: carving out an hour of your time to get your insurance sorted will show that you're an emotionally intelligent person who's willing to look after the ones you love. All with a taco in your hand. Olé!

ENTREE:

If you're over the age of 30, or you're earning over $90 000 as a single person or over $180 000 as a family, chances are you need private health insurance. If this is you, here's what I want you to do:

Pull out your phone and go to PrivateHealth.gov.au, the government healthcare search engine, to compare policies.

You want:

- hospital-only cover (do not purchase extras or 'combined' healthcare cover)

- top level cover

- a $500 excess (because you've got Mojo, baby)

- to make a co-payment for each day you spend in hospital (because it'll reduce your premium).

This search will take you less time to finish than that beer in front of you, and it should not only save you a fortune but ensure you and your family get great cover.

MAIN COURSE:

Do you have a family that relies on your income?

Ring your super fund and talk to an insurance professional, right now. Use the script on page 42.

Want to save money on your insurance bills so you can afford a year's worth of luxury massages (or some Botox, and a bit of a nip and tuck)? Use the script on page 39 while you chow down on your burrito.

DESSERT:

Skip the dessert and head back home for a bit of (cough, cough) SBS. 'Mummy and Daddy have been grown-ups on this Barefoot Date Night, so they're going to do what grown-ups do.'

Well, that's your third Barefoot Date Night done—and your insurance is now under your thumb.

Okay, you've been doing a lot of heavy lifting in the past few weeks—setting up your bank accounts, sorting your super and being a responsible little Vegemite with your insurance—so up next I've got a real treat for you.

You're about to read the most important section in the entire book:

I'm going to get you to look at your 'stuff' in an entirely different light.

See, if you're going to live a life on your terms—where you're totally in control—you're going to have to think differently from that insecure teenager in your old school photo.

This cuts to the heart of what being Barefoot is all about: I'm going to show you how to become conscious about what you spend your dough on.

No, that doesn't mean you need to become a stingy tight-arse who lives life with a clenched fist.

Hell no.

In fact, just the opposite.

I'm about to show you how you can live like a multimillionaire on a below-average income, today.

Plus, we're going to do something about your underwear.

Read on.

How to live like a multimillionaire right now

Standing in front of our burnt-out home with my wife and our little baby was the worst moment of my life. Yet to the guy at my insurance company it was just another Monday morning.

Now, you'd think his job would be to pay us our money.

In fact, his job was to pay out as little as possible—or at least hold onto the cash for as long as he could.

The conversation went something like this…

> **Insurance rep:** So you just need to let us know when you've found a builder because we can help you with your scheduled payments and…
>
> **Barefoot:** That's not needed. I'd just like my payout. In full.
>
> **Insurance rep:** What we do is hold onto the money and work with you to…
>
> **Barefoot:** Every last cent. In my hand. By the end of the week.
>
> **Insurance rep:** Oh…kay.

A week later, Liz and I sat in our rented house, on our rented couch, drinking wine out of coffee mugs.

Earlier in the day the cheque had arrived from the insurance company.

It was indeed a bloody big cheque.

I was half expecting it to be delivered by an armoured truck. A big, burly bloke with a pistol, a moustache and a steely gaze would knock authoritatively on the door. He'd open the briefcase that was handcuffed to his arm only after we'd given him the secret handshake. And then a golden light would appear as we opened the briefcase.

Nope.

Cliff the postie stuffed the letter into the postbox of our rental on Tuesday afternoon—a dot matrix printout cheque in exchange for everything we'd ever owned.

We sat there staring at the cheque, slurping our wine in silence.

'We'll go to Harvey Norman,' my wife announced.

I responded by rolling my eyes like a 13-year-old girl. For years I've stubbornly maintained a futile vendetta over Hardly Normal's 'NO DEPOSIT, NOTHING TO PAY TILL 2078!' style of marketing.

'I'm sorry, honey, but I won't go,' I told her firmly.

So the next day, as we entered our local Harvey Norman store, a saleswoman casually asked my wife, 'Are you looking for something in particular, or just browsing?'

'Well, we lost our home in a bushfire, so we have to replace everything,' said Liz.

'Everything?' quizzed the saleswoman.

'Everything,' Liz confirmed, staring blankly at the electrical goods section.

'Oh, that is … shocking,' said the saleswoman as her eyes darted excitedly around the showroom floor. 'Have you seen our dining tables? They're amazing—and they'd go beautifully with this matching lounge suite.'

'Well, we do need a dining table … and a lounge suite,' agreed Liz.

'No, no, no!' I snapped, giving the saleswoman the stink eye.

When we were safely back in the Toyota, we both agreed we'd been a little premature. After all, we didn't have a home, let alone cupboards, to put anything in yet.

So, for the next 12 months we bought pretty much…nothing.

Huh?

Yes, the bulk of the cash sat in our (high-interest online Mojo) account.

Perhaps if you were in our situation you would have shopped till you dropped. After all, it's called retail *therapy* for a reason, right?

Well, when you lose everything you own, it changes the way you think about 'stuff'. How could it not?

Now, you could set fire to your home and all your possessions to experience this epiphany…though there are less expensive (and less traumatic) ways to get to the same place.

Like learning from me.

Back to the future

I'm a huge fan of the 1980s movie franchise *Back to the Future*.

For anyone under the age of 30, the movie follows Marty McFly (Michael J. Fox) as he uses a time machine to go back to 1955 to ensure his parents hook up, and then into the future (amusingly, to 2015, when they predicted we'd all get around on hoverboards) to see what effect this would have.

Our *Back to the Future* moment was getting that bloody big cheque for everything we'd ever bought. So, with only the clothes on our back, but with the cash back in our pockets, would we do things differently?

Yes, we would.

The job of replacing everything for a family home was like doing a university degree in spending.

And over the next two years of study we realised that much of the 'stuff' we previously owned was inconsequential, just cluttering up our space. So we didn't bother replacing it.

Yet we also realised that there were things—sometimes small, sometimes large—that make a big difference to our lives. And not only did we replace them, we consciously spent more money buying them than we had before.

What I discovered was this: if you're earning over $75000 a year, you can live just as well as a multimillionaire does. And in a moment, I'll prove it to you.

But first, let's look at why you don't feel like Richie Rich right now.

Jerry Seinfeld talks garbage

You may have read that Australia has the highest rate of household debt in the world.

Yet our massive debts are just a symptom of the real problem: our out-of-control spending. Did you know that Australians on average live in the biggest homes in the world? Our supersized McMansions are 10 per cent bigger than the Yanks' (our nearest competitor in the battle of the housing bulge).

Is it because we have bigger families?

No.

Is it because we have more room to build?

No.

(If you've ever been to a house-and-land package estate, you'll see that the houses are huge and they take up almost every inch of the block—and they're packed in like sardines.)

My theory is that we live in the biggest homes in the world because we need every inch of floor space to store our 'stuff'.

And then some.

See, there's only so much room in our closets, cupboards and garages to hoard all our stuff, so, increasingly, we store our excess stuff in storage. The self-storage business is booming—there are now over 1000 centres across the country.

To paraphrase Jerry Seinfeld:

> Your home is a garbage-processing centre: when you buy new things, you're excited. So you open it on the kitchen table, then play with it in the living room.

> And then some time goes by. And you realise you're not that interested in it anymore. So you take it from the living room and stuff it in a cupboard or a drawer...that's why we have them, to hide all our mistakes and the money we've blown.

And from there it goes to the garage. Understand that no object has ever made it out of the garage and back to the house. In fact 'garage' seems to be a form of the word 'garbage'.

Speaking of garbage, it's not surprising that we're also one of the biggest waste producers in the world—second only to the United States—on a per-person basis. Between 1997 and 2007 the volume of waste produced went from 1200 kilograms to 2100 kilograms per person, according to the ABS.

Environment Victoria says the vast majority of what we buy ends up in landfill within six weeks of purchase.

December 26th (Boxing Day sales)

February 6th

Yes, I'm a part-time farmer, and I care about our environment.

But I'm also a full-time finance guy, and when I look at this photo I can't help but think of the millions of hours people worked to buy the stuff that's now rotting in a giant hole. They traded precious hours with their families and friends—hours they'll never get back—just so they could buy crap they'd eventually toss out.

Look at the picture again.

Everything you're wearing right now will eventually end up in that hole (or, at best, in recycling). Everything you purchase this year will eventually end up in that hole.

Stop for a moment and look around your room: it'll all end up in that hole too. Think about all the time you've spent working for all the stuff in your living room. Think about all the money you've spent.

Here are a couple of other questions for you:

Almost everything you've ever pined for in the past, you've now got. Think back to something you really, really lusted over. Maybe it was a car. Maybe it was a new outfit. How do you feel about it today?

And what did you purchase five years ago that still gives you genuine happiness today? (You can't really remember anything, can you?)

Truth is, for the millions of dollars most people spend over their lifetime, they get to the end of it and can count the truly meaningful things they've bought on one hand. I know this because my job puts me in contact with people who are dying, and therefore trying to sort out their affairs.

That's when people have complete clarity … often for the first time.

When it's too late.

How much is enough?

So when do we ever have enough 'stuff'?

Never.

That's not how the game works.

According to AdAge, marketers spent one *thousand* billion dollars (that's $1 trillion) globally in 2015 trying to convince us to spend. Make no mistake, when an industry spends one *thousand* billion dollars a year on *messaging*, they want a return. This is a deadly serious business.

Marketing is manipulation. Its chief aim is to create a big enough emotional void within you that you'll pull out your plastic card and swipe. It creates the void in subtle ways, mostly by reinforcing the feeling that you're dissatisfied with what you already have.

And it works like magic.

In his book *Affluenza*, author Clive Hamilton states:

> Sixty-two per cent of Australians believe they cannot afford to buy everything they really need. When we consider that Australia is one of the world's richest countries and that Australians today have incomes *three times higher* than in 1950, it is remarkable that so many people feel their incomes are inadequate.

In other words, you and I won the lifestyle lotto! Not only are we lucky enough to be living in the wealthiest period in history, we're also living in the richest nation in the world, according to Credit Suisse.

And yet, to quote comedian Louis CK, 'everything's amazing and everyone is miserable'.

Economist Arun Abey—in his book *How Much is Enough?*—says our prosperity has come with baggage:

> Youth and adult suicide rates have doubled or tripled over the past forty years. The biggest-selling drugs are those treating depression, anxiety and stress. The onset of depression now occurs at age fourteen, anxiety at age eleven. Obesity and diabetes have reached epidemic proportions.

It's only when you start to see through the brainwashing—all the millions of manipulative marketing messages that are pointed right at you, and make the decision not to buy into it—that you're truly free to tread your own path.

Just a little bit more

I know what you're thinking: 'Sure, marketing is bulldust...but I'd still be happy with more money'.

Okay, so how much more would you need?

I've asked thousands of people this question—people of all ages and income levels—and they all give pretty much the same answer: 'more than I'm earning right now'.

It is never enough.

Case in point: a 2014 survey by News Ltd of 50 000 Aussies found that 53 per cent of people earning $200 000 a year felt either 'angry' or 'frustrated' at their cost of living.

Time out.

Let's get some perspective.

The average wage in Australia is $81 530, according to the ABS. If you plug that into globalrichlist.com it shows that you're in the top 0.27 per cent of the richest people in the world by income. Yes, even on the average Aussie wage you're richer than 99.72 per cent of the global population.

Yet here's the thing:

Losing everything didn't turn Liz and me into Buddhist monks, swearing off all material possessions.

And it didn't turn us into tightwads. You may get your rocks off cleaning your windows with potatoes, hitchhiking to work or recycling your bathwater for soup stock. We're just not wired that way. We're not misers.

What the process of losing everything did teach us was the art of *conscious spending*.

In other words, we think about the things that genuinely make our lives more meaningful, or more comfortable, and we spend extravagantly on them, guilt-free. At the same time, we look at the stuff that we buy unconsciously and ruthlessly cut it out.

If I were to make it more 'Twittery', I'd say:

'Spend your $$ on the stuff you love—cut out the waste.'

I know what you're thinking:

'Nice little concept you got there, cobber, but where's that multimillion-dollar lifestyle you promised me?'

Alright, so let me show you how you can live like a multimillionaire on a below-average income, today.

#BarefootRich

My first major purchase after the fire was a pillow.

Seriously, a pillow.

It's a great practical example of conscious spending.

Your noggin lies on a pillow for a third of your life. That's a long time to put up with a bad pillow.

When my sister got divorced, I bought her a pillow.

Then I circled it out to my staff. I bought them pillows as well.

Hyungtak, my Korean graphic designer, was admittedly a little perplexed with my offer. He kind of bowed graciously and carried the pillow under his arm on the tram home.

I can only imagine the discussion he had with his girlfriend (also Korean) when he arrived home to his studio apartment:

'Is this some sort of Australian employment custom?' she asks.

'I have no idea,' he replies. 'Scott speaks with such a thick Australian accent that I really only understand every third word he says.'

'You don't think he … *likes* you … do you?' she says.

'No, I don't think so. He gave pillows to the rest of the team as well.'

Anyhow, if you haven't bought a pillow in the past 12 months, you need to.

A UK study in 2011 found that 'up to a third of the weight of your pillow could be made up of bugs, dead skin, and house dust mites and their faeces'.

Sweet dreams!

And you know what, you should buy *this* pillow: it's called the Dunlopillo, and it's the Mercedes-Benz of pillows. (Just to reiterate, I get zero kickbacks for recommending this product—I just like it.)

James Packer is a multibillionaire, and yet he still puts his head on a pillow for eight hours a night just like you do. Anyway, I reckon this is the pillow he'd use. Bang for your buck-wise, this is an awesome purchase that makes you feel wealthy as you drift off to sleep.

Socks and jocks

Yes, this is officially the only finance book that's ever spoken about investing in underwear.

FAMILY JEWELS SHOULDN'T BE HOUSED IN A SLUM.

SAY NO TO DODGY UNDIES

BONDS

Right now at the bottom of your undies and socks draw there are at least a few pairs you avoid wearing—maybe the elastic's gone, or your pinky (toe) pokes out or they're just plain uncomfortable. I want you to put down this book and throw them out. All of them. Go on. Do it now. They're just clutter.

Then it's time to treat yourself and buy some 'lucky' undies and socks—ones you enjoy putting on, that make you feel comfy.

Weird?

Maybe, though I would remind you that you're reading a finance book from a guy who doesn't wear shoes, so we're in this together. Besides, people can justify spending $8000 to upgrade to business class for a 14-hour flight. Why not fly business class in your undies every day?

Your car

Most people get screwed when they buy a new car.

And that's mainly because most people suck at thinking through the alternatives.

Here's an example:

The difference between the base model Holden Commodore and the top-of-the-range model is around $15000. What do you get for that? Leather seats, a nicer stereo, some faux woodgrain inserts in the dash and a wankier-sounding name.

With the help of a salesperson, most people are unconsciously lured into buying the more expensive model. That makes perfect sense—after all, that's how we've been trained to think (more expensive = better).

However, a conscious spender sees $15000 in a different context. To a conscious spender $15000 represents:

- a year's worth of petrol, insurance, registration and pine-tree air-fresheners

or...

- a dirty weekend away each month for a year (with spa treatments), an award-winning Sonos sound system, a Grand Master bed (the highest rated bed online), luxury Boll & Branch linen (highest grade, long-staple organic cotton), a Dunlopillo (as used by James Packer), and eight pairs of ultra-comfy Bonds socks and jocks.

Guess which one I'd go for?

My Barefoot Steps are going to provide you with the financial control to handle whatever life throws up at you. But that doesn't mean you have to be a miserable tight-arse.

The truth is you can live like a multimillionaire today by cutting back on meaningless crap and diverting your spending to the little luxuries you use every day. (Seriously, get the freaking pillow, it's like a day spa for your face each night.)

Okay, so now that you've learned about the mindset you need to consciously spend your money, let me show you how to automate it.

STEP 2

SET UP YOUR BUCKETS

This Barefoot Step is where the rubber hits the road: It's what I call my 'Serviette Strategy'. It's a simple, three-'bucket' solution where you put your money on autopilot so you'll never have to worry about it again.

Plus, I'll explain the specific way I want you to manage your money as a couple, including a pre-set spending limit so you'll end up having more pillow fights than money fights.

The Serviette Strategy

Date: 1 November 2012

Location: Romsey Pub (Romsey, Victoria)

'Here's how we're going to manage our money,' I announced to Liz (on our very own Barefoot Date Night).

'Oh really?' she said, eyebrows raised, head cocked to one side.

See, during the years that Liz and I had been 'living in sin', as my grandmother put it, we'd kept our money separate, splitting things roughly down the middle.

But a month out from our wedding I knew it was time to have 'the talk'.

To succeed over the long term, I knew I had to come up with a simple, hassle-free plan that operated on autopilot (for Liz) yet moved us forward and built our wealth (for me).

'You're talking about putting us on a budget, aren't you?' said Liz, folding her arms.

'Well…'

'Let's get one thing straight right here. I will not have you dictating every last dollar we spend,' she declared, giving me a factor-10 stink eye.

We are not stingy people. You know the type: they never bring wine or beer when they come for dinner (but always happily drink yours). They often complain about the cost of their kids' (free, public) schooling. And they put in the exact change when you're out to dinner: 'Our mains were cheaper, so our share of the bill is … $45.40' (and then they put in $45 and four 10-cent pieces).

I assured Liz that I wasn't advocating we cut our own hair or wear acid-wash jeans from Best & Less (though it really is only a matter of time before they come back into style), and I certainly wasn't suggesting we follow a strict budget.

Honestly, I've never been able to stick to one. The few times I tried, I found the process of tracking every last dollar on a spreadsheet overwhelming. Besides, I was fairly sure the only time my bride had looked at a spreadsheet was when she accidently clicked 'Excel' instead of 'iTunes'.

This is obviously going to be a crushing disappointment to financial nerds everywhere, who were expecting me to advocate for something like this:

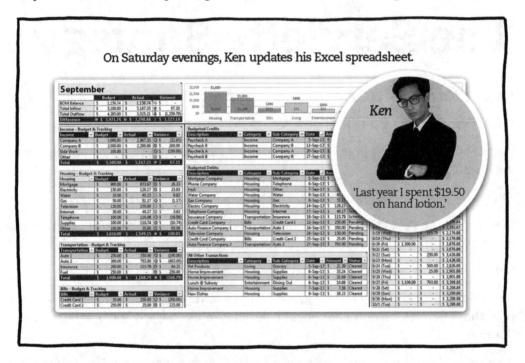

On Saturday evenings, Ken updates his Excel spreadsheet.

Ken

'Last year I spent $19.50 on hand lotion.'

Instead I decided to make it so simple that I could draw our plan on the back of a serviette.

Introducing the Serviette Strategy

Before the parma came, but after the calamari rings, we'd agreed on the three things we really wanted from our money.

Top of our list?

To be totally financially secure.

Which made sense. After all, we were about to get hitched and we were already pregnant (scandal!).

And, according to Relationships Australia, the biggest cause of relationship breakdowns is fights about money (and monogamy, but mainly money).

The second thing we valued was the freedom to travel at least once a year, and to enjoy nice dinners out with family and friends.

The third thing was to build our wealth over the long term, so we could wind down working sooner rather than later. (Okay, if I'm being really honest, Liz was kind of like 'meh' about the exciting world of long-term investing... but she understood it came with the territory when she married the Barefoot Investor.)

It was my time to shine.

With one final swig of Carlton Draught for courage, I pulled out a pen and drew our new financial plan on the back of a pub serviette.

Here's what I drew:

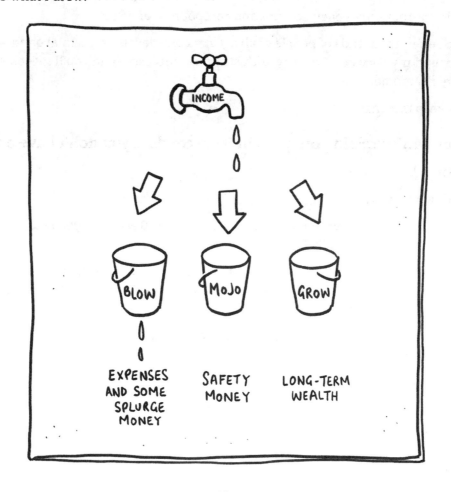

Yes, our entire money management plan consists of dividing our income into three 'buckets':

- a *Blow* Bucket, for daily expenses, the occasional splurge and some extra cash to fight financial fires

- a *Mojo* Bucket, to provide some 'safety money'

- a *Grow* Bucket, to build long-term wealth and total security.

You remember those everyday transaction accounts and online saver accounts you set up on your first Barefoot Date Night? Well, the Serviette Strategy is going to put them to work. So read on...

Don't for a moment be fooled by the simplicity of the picture. Liz and I have used this plan to manage our investment property, save for our honeymoon, pay off our mortgage, manage a business that earns income in inconsistent lumps, create a solid-as-a-rock emergency account and compound our wealth.

Even better: thousands of people of all ages, income levels and sexual orientations have used my Serviette Strategy with stunning success—and you'll meet some of them in a moment.

Let's keep moving.

If you can't explain your plan in 30 seconds...you don't have a plan

It's kinda basic, right?

That's why it works.

If you can't explain how you manage your money in 30 seconds, you're not going to stick with it—and good luck trying to get your partner on board.

Look, I've helped thousands of people with their money and I can tell you that the conventional wisdom espoused by finance experts—'Get on a budget! Track your spending'—is dead wrong.

Using *willpower* to force yourself to stick to a rigid budget, day in day out, just doesn't work.

In fact, it's the opposite.

If you really want to win, you should ditch tracking everything and instead simplify your choices.

Barack Obama gets it: 'You'll see I wear only grey or blue suits', he explained to author Michael Lewis. 'I don't want to make decisions about what I'm eating or wearing because I have too many other decisions to make.'

American social psychologist Roy Baumeister backs him up. Baumeister famously found that willpower is like a muscle that becomes fatigued from overuse. Basically, his research suggests that willpower is a limited resource.

Baumeister says that people who succeed don't have more willpower than you: they just develop better daily routines and habits, which after a while become automatic and require less thought—less conscious energy.

And that right there is the power of implementing my Serviette Strategy.

Let's grab a bucket (or three).

The Blow Bucket

Most people only have one money bucket.

If you're renting, it's your transaction account. If you own a home, it might be your mortgage. Either way, your pay comes in, money goes out, and you 'hope' some is left over to put towards investing and saving.

And then old Fido finally catches that car. D'oh! Vet bills.

And then an unexpected emergency: Christmas. Ho! Ho! D'oh!

There's nothing systematic about it.

Even worse?

Your Blow Bucket has a hole in it: every dollar of income you pour into it leaks out the bottom.

This is just as true for a uni student blowing their Austudy on a pub crawl as it is for 90s rapper MC Hammer, who squandered his $30 million fortune on fancy (leased) cars, a thirsty entourage and (my personal favourite) gold-plated 'Hammertime' gates for his home. ('U can't touch this'—apparently his creditors could.)

The deal with the Blow Bucket is spending more money on the stuff you love and less on the stuff you don't. Better yet, with this plan you'll actually allocate some of your pay packet to guilt-free splurges for stuff that'll put a smile on your dial.

The Barefoot benchmark: live off 60 per cent of your income

So how much does it cost you to keep the lights running and the kids from drinking out of the dog's bowl? In other words, how much does it cost to run 'You, Inc.'?

Well, a good yardstick is allocating 60 per cent of your take-home pay (that is, your after-tax household income) to food, shelter and Netflix—all the things you need to live safely in the suburbs.

Here are some rough percentages based on an average household income:

- housing (rent or home loan*): 30 per cent

- utilities (power, gas, water, broadband, phones): 5–10 per cent

- transport: 5–10 per cent

- insurance: 5 per cent

- food: 5–10 per cent.

(* If you have a home loan already, the *minimum* payments would be part of this 60 per cent in Daily Expenses. If you don't have one yet, you're going to enjoy Step 4.)

This money is going to sit in the 'Daily Expenses' transaction account that you opened in Step 1 (but just roll with me for now—soon I'll show you exactly what each of those accounts will be used for).

Hang on. I know what you're thinking.

Sure, these percentages would work for people on an average income, but they'd blow out for people on a really low income (more of their money would go towards food and shelter), and for those on a really high income (BMWs, baby!).

That's true. It's just a guide. You should work it out to suit your income. (And reduce your living expenses wherever you can.)

And what about if you're on a variable income (business owners, freelancers and the like)?

You've just described me. My solution is to keep my fixed expenses as low as possible. And for my business I have a monthly amount I know I have to earn in order to pay my bills. That gives me a baseline to hit to keep all my automatic payments going.

The Mojo Bucket

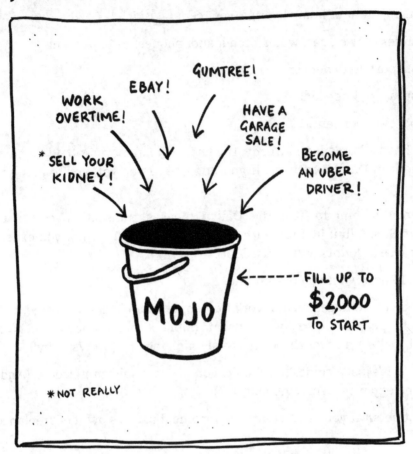

The aim of the Mojo Bucket is to get your Mojo back, baby.

You know the feeling—it's a spring in your step that says, 'I don't stress about money'.

Now, you shouldn't keep your Mojo in an offset account or a redraw facility attached to your mortgage, and you shouldn't link it to your everyday transaction account. This is the *totally separate*, high-interest online savings account that we named 'Mojo' in Step 1—the one you opened up with $2000, remember?

You only touch it in emergencies, like losing your job or getting sick...or your house burning down.

(Tickets to Gaga are not an emergency.)

Sadly, most people never experience the feeling of Mojo.

A survey by comparison site finder.com.au found that 30 per cent of Aussies have less than $1000 available to deal with an emergency.

Stressful?

You don't know the half of it.

Professor Bob Cummins and his researchers from Deakin University found that financial stress produces feelings similar to physical torture. (I would have loved to be a participant in Bob's experiment: 'Savings or an electric shock? You decide'.)

My direct experience of advising thousands of people over many years has left me in no doubt about the life-changing benefits of Mojo.

And remember, if you don't have a spare $2000 to put into your brand-new Mojo account, do whatever you can to find this money. Flog stuff on Gumtree, put in overtime at work, sell your kidney.

The Grow Bucket

The third and final bucket I drew for Liz was the Grow Bucket.

The guts of it is this: if you want to stay poor, focus on spending your money. If you want to become wealthy, focus on saving and investing your money.

The aim of the Grow Bucket is to get a little wealthier every day.

Every dollar you pour into the Grow Bucket should double every seven to 10 years (in boom times it'll be quicker; in bad times it'll be slower). It's not exactly quick, but over your life it can make you incredibly wealthy.

Your Grow Bucket includes your brand-new, ultra-low-cost super fund and any other investments you own (like shares, investment property or education savings for your kids). As we work our way through the Barefoot Steps, the Grow Bucket will take centre stage, but right now it's more than enough just to have your super sorted (which you did in Step 1)—in fact, with that you're ahead of 95 per cent of investors.

Manage your money in 10 minutes a week

So that's what I drew for Liz.

She sat there, surveying the serviette.

'I like it, Mister Pape.'

Success!

See, in any relationship there's usually someone who's really interested in money (and given that you're reading this book, that would be you), while the other partner's idea of a savings plan is to buy a slab instead of a six pack.

Yet with the simplicity of our Serviette Strategy, Liz and I have been able to manage our money in around 10 minutes a week. We're both on the same page, and we both understand exactly where our income is going, and why.

Putting it all together: Serviette Strategy + your new accounts = happiness

Remember those five accounts we set up on your very first Barefoot Date Night?

Well, now we're going to put it all together with the Serviette Strategy, so you can automate your money.

Set up payment to your Daily Expenses account

Tell your employer (in writing) that you've changed bank accounts.

If you're following along with the picture on page 65, you'll see that your Daily Expenses account (everyday transaction account) is essentially your Blow Bucket.

Your employer needs to put 100 per cent of your take-home pay into this account.

Then I want you to try and live off the Barefoot Benchmark of 60 per cent of your take-home pay. Remember, this is bare-bones living expenses (think shelter, groceries and bills). Leave that 60 per cent in your Daily Expenses account for, well, daily expenses.

What about the other 40 per cent?

That's why I got you to set up three other accounts—Splurge, Smile and Fire Extinguisher.

(By the way, you should keep all your old accounts open for the next month or so—with $500 in them—while you change over all your direct debits. If you call your bank they'll give you a list of all your direct debits and your new bank should help you get it rearranged. After that, ditch the old accounts.)

Let's roll.

Set up payment to your Splurge account

You are hereby directed to go out and blow 10 per cent of your money on anything that makes you feel good (shoes, booze, lattes—whatever).

This is what your Splurge account (the other everyday transaction account) is for.

Set up an automatic transfer of 10 per cent of your take-home pay from your Daily Expenses account into your Splurge account, each time you're paid.

And remember, your Splurge account has its own ATM card (see Step 1) so you can easily whip it out and buy beers for your mates when it's your turn.

I suggest you keep this at the front of your wallet and mark it SPLURGE with a Sharpie.

One other thing to remember: when your Splurge money for the month is gone, it's gone—you can't cut into your other accounts.

Set up payment to your Smile account

Another 10 per cent of your take-home pay should be automatically transferred from Daily Expenses to Smile (online saver).

This is not for splurging when you feel like it; it's for big goals that will take longer to save up for. Overseas holidays, weddings, divorces—anything that is going to cost more than a few weeks' wages.

I call it the Smile account because every time you think of what you're saving up for, you smile.

Now, 10 per cent is a ballpark figure. You can be a bit more scientific than that. Just think about the big goals you have over the next 12 months and chunk them down into monthly amounts (or whatever your pay cycle is). If a holiday's going to cost you $6000, say, then that's $500 each month ($6000 divided by 12).

Whatever figure you come up with for your Smile account, you'll need to adjust your living expenses accordingly to make it work.

Set up your Fire Extinguisher account

Finally, allocate 20 per cent of your take-home pay from Daily Expenses to your Fire Extinguisher account (online saver). Again, make it automatic with a direct transfer every time you get paid.

You see, you're going to use it to put out financial fires.

What's a financial fire?

It could be your crushing credit card debt.

It could be the home deposit you're saving up for.

It could be paying off your mortgage.

And that's the point—your Fire Extinguisher account will be used for *different* financial fires at different times in your life. The 20 per cent amount won't change, but what you use it for will.

But don't worry about the details right now. As we move through the Barefoot Steps I'll tell you precisely where to point your Fire Extinguisher—and when.

Putting it all together

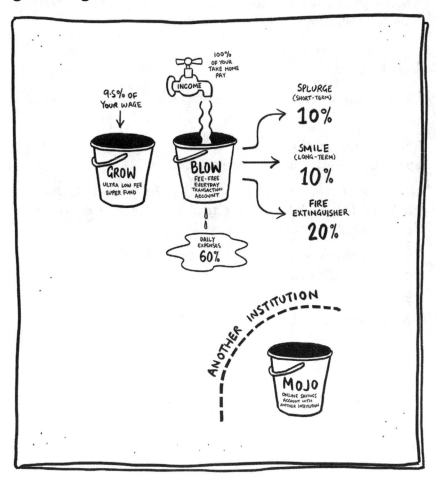

BAREFOOT DATE NIGHT MENU

Week 4

Tonight, you're going to run the numbers for your household. Knowing how much it costs to run 'You, Inc.'—actually having a monthly dollar figure—is powerful.

ENTREE:

Get out your phone and calculate 60 per cent of your take-home pay.

This is your Barefoot Benchmark—how much you *should* be spending on bare-bones living expenses.

Next, work out what it actually costs to be you (think shelter, groceries and bills). If it's more than your Barefoot Benchmark figure, look at ways to cut costs.

Finally, calculate your 10–10–20 figures (10 per cent of your take-home pay to Splurge, 10 per cent to Smile, and 20 per cent to Fire Extinguisher).

Now you have your numbers, we're going to get crafty.

MAIN COURSE:

I want you to draw your own serviette, right here.

Put in your numbers, name your accounts, and actually see where your money is going.

Now you have a simple, visual plan.

Now you are in control.

DRAW YOUR OWN SERVIETTE STRATEGY

DESSERT:

If you're single? Order whatever the hell you want.

If you're married? One plate, two spoons. (Get used to it.)

Next up, we're going to work out who taught you about money (and what their agenda was), and I'll show you the fastest way to become debt free once and for all.

STEP 3

DOMINO YOUR DEBTS

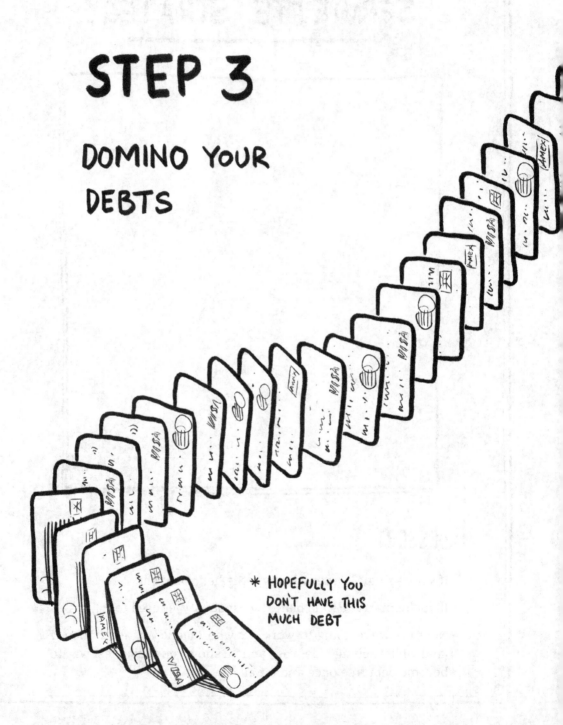

* HOPEFULLY YOU DON'T HAVE THIS MUCH DEBT

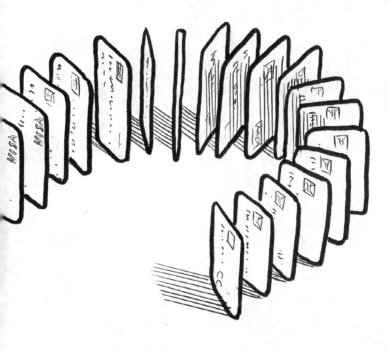

I'm about to show you how to turn the process of paying off your debts into a game of dominoes—it's the fastest way I know to escape the cult of credit once and for all. But first, let me explain why there's a good chance your primary school sold you into a life of debt...

Removing the brainwashing

The senator swivelled back in his chair, sizing me up.

Clearly, I'd pissed him off.

I was sitting before the Senate Parliamentary Inquiry into credit cards.

It was all fairly tame, as these things tend to be. Other financial experts, mainly old white blokes with far less hair than me (think Kochie), had given their evidence, pointing out things like:

- Credit cards charge rip-off interest rates. (Boo!)
- Australia has the highest rate of household debt in the world. (Hiss!)
- And, doncha know, the banks make a lot of money out of credit cards? (Yawn...)

Yet the government doesn't need to spend millions of bucks to work out that credit cards are a rip-off.

So when it was my turn to front the Inquiry, I said something that I knew would make the newspapers the next day:

> Having the Commonwealth Bank—the nation's largest issuer of credit cards—in our schools teaching kids about money is like having Ronald McDonald teaching our kids about nutrition.

'Cough, cough,' went the senator.

'Scribble, scribble,' went the press.

I proceeded to explain how Australia's biggest bank has ruthlessly bought its way into classrooms, then used its position to build a multibillion-dollar credit card marketing database.

Sure, it may begin with a cute little plastic money box…but the truth is that the only plastic present CommBank cares about is the credit card their marketing database automatically offers kids on their 18th birthday.

Juicy stuff.

The senator, who was looking down his nose at me, knew it as well. Now I can't be sure, but I suspect that over his parliamentary career he'd spent quite a bit of time with banking lobbyists. So I decided to turn the tables and ask him the same question I'll ask you:

Who taught you about money?

Stop for a moment and answer that question: who taught you about money?

If you were lucky, your parents were financially savvy. Yet the research suggests that the odds of that happening are fairly low. In fact, there's a better chance that you learned what *not* to do by watching your parents.

And if you didn't learn about money at home, you probably learned about it at school…courtesy of the Commonwealth Bank. The CBA's School Banking Program, known as 'Dollarmites', is an Aussie institution that's been around for over 80 years and is currently in more than 2500 primary schools across the country.

Remember that cute little savings passbook account you were given in primary school? I'm sure you do.

What you probably didn't realise is just how cut-throat it is for the bank to get into your classroom.

Here's how they do it.

The CBA pays cash-strapped schools a $5 kickback for every kid they sign up, plus a 5 per cent commission on whatever the child deposits (up to $10), with 'a minimum commission payment of $25 per quarter'.

Does that sound familiar?

Replace 'schools' with 'financial advisors' and you've got the exact recipe the CBA has used for years to make billions of dollars from its customers. As we have seen, the Royal Commission has labelled CBA a 'gold medal winner' for charging dead people advice fees, and has uncovered shocking fraud, forgery and cover-ups in the bank's financial planning department.

Does that sound like the sort of institution that should be teaching kids about money?

Well, along with student bank accounts, the CBA has developed a huge syllabus of branded 'financial education programs' that teachers are encouraged to use in their classrooms.

Schools greet them with open arms and freely pass around their marketing material, complete with corporate-coloured cartoon characters that teach the kids about managing money ... or at least the bank's way of managing money.

My favourite CommBank cartoon character is 'Cred' (pictured).

'Cred's a cool dude,' says the CBA.

(Though he also has out-of-control credit card debt, which means that for the past 11 days he's eaten every meal from a tin can and had to Gumtree his skateboard to pay the rent.)

I like to think of Cred as the Marlboro Man for the new generation of kids.

Hey kids! Wanna be a cool dude like Cred?

Well get a mothertrucker of a credit balance, and don't pay it off ... thumbs up!

Are you smelling bulldust right now?

What are the chances that the CBA-prepared financial education program teaches kids that credit cards are dangerous? Or that car loans in your 20s will rob you in your 30s and 40s? Or that you should shop around to get a better deal?

Zero.

Even the name of the card is a con. A 'credit' card has positive connotations. After all, who doesn't want to be given credit for something? What it really is, is a 'debt' card… though I assume that name was voted down in the marketing brainstorming session.

When I teach kids about money in schools, I give them a simple message: debt cards make everything more expensive. And if they get out of hand, they destroy your self-confidence.

Achieving a sense of financial control isn't about your net worth—it's about your self-worth.

That's why I refuse to have a credit card. But you've probably got one.

So let's talk about it.

Your first credit card

Think back to your first credit card. Not the loaner from your parents. The one with your name on it.

How old were you?

If you're like most people, you were still a teenager, fresh out of school.

Maybe it came courtesy of the Dollarmites database, or perhaps it was included in your 'youth banking package', which the banks will typically offer when you go to university or get your first job.

The banks generally include a credit card with a low balance, 'just to tide you over in an emergency' (like student night at the pub). Then they keep 'rewarding you' with increases to your limit, so long as you keep spending.

In that way they're kind of like a drug pusher who gives you your first taste for free, knowing they'll make their money back a hundred times over. But that's not how most kids view their first credit card. That's because the bank presents it something like this:

> We've done our research on you, Johnnie, and we like what we see. We think you're a fine, upstanding young person, so we will entrust you with our precious money. You can spend it on whatever you please. Just don't leave home without it, because if there's an emergency you'll need it.

That sounds incredibly lame. No-one really thinks like that… right?

Wrong.

Most teenagers do. And when your first credit card turned up in the mail, you probably did too.

And that explains why financial institutions the world over are increasingly targeting ever-younger kids. My favourite is the Hello Kitty Platinum Plus Visa Credit Card, which the company believes 'resonates with their target audience', which is…eight-year-old girls!

Vodka, Visa and vomit

There's a good chance your first experience with a credit card worked out about as successfully as your first foray with vodka…passing out in a toilet with vomit all over you.

Yet the difference is that a financial hangover can last for years.

If you only pay off the minimum on a $4400 credit card debt, it'll take you:

31 years to pay off…and $12 924 in interest.

And that's only if you stop spending money on it. In reality, the bank will keep increasing your limit. Which means you can keep spending right through your 20s (and sometimes your 30s, 40s and 50s) without realising just how much you're being screwed.

And that's where I come in.

Let's you and I do a bit of roleplay.

You can be the typical Aussie with a typical $4200 credit card debt, and I'll be the Barefoot Investor.

> **Here's me:** So, what did you spend the $4200 on?
>
> **Here's you:** Havaianas.
>
> **Here's me:** As in thongs? Or Cuban cigars? Dude, what the hell are you smoking?

I've been asking people the 'what did you spend it on' question for many years and I've never had anyone nail it correctly.

There are two reasons for this:

First, getting a credit card is like buying a dog. Once you get the card, the banks know it's rare that you'll give it up (which is why there's a good chance you've got an updated version of your first card sitting in your wallet right now...only with a much higher limit). It can bite you, urinate all over your couch, dump a turd in the middle of your lounge room and you'll still keep it. In fact, after a while your credit card limit starts to feel like *your* money.

Second, the biggest purchase you make on your credit card is interest. Make no bones about it, the game is designed that way. Credit cards are compound interest in reverse: they're designed to blow out and grow bigger and bigger, even if you stop spending. That's why they set the minimum monthly repayment at 2 per cent but charge 20 per cent per annum (or more) in interest.

It begins when you're a kid and you're given your first credit card, and continues throughout your working life. And as your credit card *increases*, your self-confidence *decreases*. You look at your bill and you say to yourself, 'I'm no good with money...and I never will be'.

But that's simply not true.

Look, I've helped thousands of people get out of debt. Quickly. Painlessly. Without having to feel like they're setting out on a marathon. And I've never had anyone ever say to me, 'The worst thing I did was pay off my credit cards, you bastard'.

In fact, it's the opposite. When people cut up their credit card and post a pic on the Barefoot Facebook page, they're ecstatic! Why? Because they've finally stepped off the merry-go-round of misery and made a decision they know they'll never regret.

Being in debt is often a lonely, isolating experience. You don't tell your family or friends that you're struggling to pay off your credit cards, right? It'd be a downer. Embarrassing too. I mean, everyone knows they're a rip-off! What the hell's wrong with you?

So you just trudge on, keeping a running balance in your head. Occasionally it goes down, and you get your hopes up...but before long it's back up to its limit. Most people live like this for their entire working lives, and end up paying the banks the equivalent of a house deposit for the privilege.

You can block it out for a while and pretend it doesn't matter.

After all, in this country, if you're normal, you're broke.

But I've never wanted to be normal, and that's why I cut up my credit cards years ago.

And to quote the ad…it was 'priceless'.

Stand for something

I run a business, a farm and a family—all without a credit card.

Yes, there's a sense of relief from never having to worry about getting hit with the fees and charges, but truthfully, the main reason is how it makes me feel.

I see not having a credit card as a *reverse status symbol*: I'm showing people that I don't need one. Kids learn by watching their parents—and my kids will grow up watching their mum and dad pay their own way with cash. Seriously, how's that for the ultimate rewards program?

Okay, so by this stage of the book you're thinking…

'This dude *really* doesn't like credit cards.'

and …

'I think I'll skip over the rest of this because…*I pay my credit cards off every month and get 55 days' use of the bank's money interest free!*'

Okay, so what's 55 days of bank interest on your money worth?

About $20.

And you only get to keep that if you don't miss any repayments.

And the chances are you will, and then you'll be whacked with a backdated interest bill.

ABC News puts it like this: 'Only one-third of people believe they pay interest on their credit cards; the Australian Bureau of Statistics suggests the real figure is actually about double that'.

Barefoot puts it like this: 'So are you feeling lucky, punk?'

But 'I pay it off every month' is just one of the many things on your mind at this point. You could be thinking…

'My credit card is *great for the rewards points!*'

The truth is most people spend money they don't have to earn points they'll never use.

Almost all credit card rewards programs charge an annual fee. They start at $49 and go up to $5000 for the American Express 'I have a small penis' Centurion Card. On an average card, you'll need to spend more than $18000 a year just to break even.

The banks design rewards schemes to keep you spending, usually by capping the points you can earn over a set period. They also have a track record of dropping the value of the points each year.

The final hurdle comes in claiming your reward. It's getting harder with each passing year. A Qantas point is now reportedly worth as little as 0.6 cents, and they've also made it harder to get a seat, restricting the number of spots allocated for frequent flyers.

Here are yet more lines people trot out about credit cards:

'What about all those other rewards?!'

Analysis by finder.com.au suggests you'd have to spend $22000 to earn a $100 gift card. An iPhone 6 requires a $370000 spend.

'My credit card gives me free travel insurance!'

Credit card insurance is worth exactly what you pay for it. I had a young couple come to me after they gave birth to a premature baby in Italy. They tried to claim it on the credit card's insurance but the claim was declined. They were left with close to a $1 million bill.

'I only use it in emergencies!'

A credit card isn't about convenience, and it sure as hell isn't about emergencies—trust me, if you're in a genuine crisis, the last people you need to call on are these vultures.

Ask your granddad how he survived genuine financial hardships without a high-interest-rate loan from a bank in his pocket.

'It's perfect for buying stuff online!'

You can use your debit card. It works exactly the same way, and it's just as secure.

'Having a credit card is great for my credit rating!'

Nope. You get a good credit rating by having a job and savings, and paying your bills on time.

'I can manage it!'

I've noticed that people who try and 'manage' their credit card debts are nearly always broke. They may be able to pay it down at times, but it always shoots back up. Why does this happen? Because they're weak-willed? Not really. It's simply because they keep their card in their wallet. That's like a drunk keeping a beer in the fridge for hot days.

'I love my platinum credit card!'

The 7-Eleven attendant isn't impressed. He thinks you're a wanker.

It's time to get real. It's time to stand for something. It's time to call your bank and say, 'Please cancel my credit card, and then change it over to a Visa or Mastercard debit card'.

'I'll never be able to pay it off…'

Nonsense.

The truth is you need to have some 'no matter whats' in your life:

- No matter what, I'm not going to take out a high-interest loan to fund crap I don't need.

- No matter what, I'm going to pay my own way, and claw back my financial confidence.

- No matter what, I'm going to set an example for the people around me.

Know this: the moment you say 'no matter what'—and really mean it—you no longer have a debt problem. You're already free.

Everything you wanted to know about paying off your debts— in one-and-a-bit pages

Should I pay off my HECS-HELP debt?

No, it'll look after itself.

Your HECS-HELP debt is not charged an interest rate. Instead, each year on 1 June it's indexed to the cost of living. In 2017 that index rate was a measly 1.5 per cent. And remember, you don't start making repayments until you earn more than $55 874. Finally, if you croak, the debt dies with you. All up that's a very sweet deal.

Bottom line: there are better things to do with your money... like the Barefoot Steps.

What should I do about my car loan?

Get rid of it.

I'm deadly serious. Don't pay interest on something that's rapidly falling in value. That doesn't mean you have to drive your kids around in a Datsun 180B. My rule of thumb is you shouldn't drive a car that's worth more than half your annual income. Buy something you can afford... with cash you've saved up.

Which credit card should I pay first?

The one with the smallest balance.

Should I consolidate my debts?

Maybe, but if you do, just make sure you only do it through a bank or a credit union (steer clear of infomercial-style spray-on-hair-in-a-can 'debt solutions' companies). And understand it's not a magic wand. What's keeping you from paying off your debts once and for all is your pattern of spending money. The people who ditch their debts for good have one thing in common: they change their attitude.

Should I worry about what's on my credit file?

Yes. But don't get all freaked out about it. Treat it like an annual sexual health check. Each year when you do your tax, you should call credit reporting agency Equifax on 13 83 32 and request a free copy of your credit report. If there's anything incorrect on your file, they have the legal obligation to correct it.

Dude, Visa has a hitman looking for me — should I go bankrupt?

I only recommend bankruptcy in the most extreme circumstances.

The *only* people I trust when it comes to advising on bankruptcy are the independent, not-for-profit financial counsellors at Financial Counselling Australia. Call them on 1800 007 007 and arrange a catch-up.

Domino your debts (except your HECS-HELP and your home)

Today is a wonderful day.

Today you're going to taste true freedom.

Today you're going to regain control of your life.

The bottom line is this: if you have a credit card debt, or a personal loan, or a car loan, you're not in control of your financial future.

You're not free.

Your debt controls every minute of your day, from the moment your phone alarm bleats and bounces around your skull first thing in the morning.

Debt is slavery.

It controls what you wear, where you work and what you eat for lunch. It never leaves you. It controls what you do on weekends, and where you go on holidays.

It colours your view of the world. It colours your view of *you* and what you're capable of—your hopes, your dreams.

Debt eats away at your self-esteem.

Look, I'm not here to judge you.

What I'm here to tell you is that if you're in debt you've already experienced the worst of it. You're about to regain a feeling of confidence and control. It's all upwards from here. My method works. It will work for you. And best of all, you're going to enjoy it.

It's like playing a game of (Debt) Dominoes.

There's a bit of work in setting it up, but it's worth it, because once you've lined everything up you'll find that each debt gets knocked down like a domino, one after the other, automatically.

There are five dominoes you need to set up to knock out your debts:

- Domino 1: Calculate
- Domino 2: Negotiate
- Domino 3: Eliminate
- Domino 4: Detonate
- Domino 5: Celebrate!

Let's do this!

Domino 1: Calculate

The first thing you need to do is line up all your debts—other than your HECS-HELP and your mortgage (if you have one, which we'll deal with in Step 4).

Here's how:

Write down all your debts—credit cards, car loans, parking fines, money you owe to friends—in the table below.

Name of debt	Total amount	Interest rate	Monthly minimum
			Total:

Research from the University of Ouyen suggests that only 0.04 per cent of readers will fill out this table.

Yet here's the thing: I've helped thousands of people get out of debt, and this plan works. There's something very powerful about getting stuff out of your head and down on paper.

Domino 2: Negotiate

Now that you've calculated all your debts, it's time to negotiate. Hard.

The first thing to do is grab your statements, ring your bank and follow this script:

> **You:** Hello! I'm looking to renegotiate my credit card. Do you have the authority to change my rate? (If they answer 'no', say 'That's fine, please transfer me to someone who does'.)
>
> **You:** G'day, my name is _____ . Who am I speaking to?
>
> **Bank rep:** Derek.
>
> **You:** Hey Derek! I've been a loyal customer of yours for __ years. I've decided that it's time I got on top of my credit card debt…it's really depressing me, Derek…you know?
>
> **Derek:** Oh! Ummm.
>
> **You:** So, I have an offer from Citibank of a zero per cent balance transfer for 18 months, with no application fees, no ongoing fees and no transfer fees. And I'd like you to match that.
>
> **Derek:** There's no way I can do that.
>
> **You:** Well, I see I'm being charged an annual fee of $__ and __ per cent. What can you do for me, Derek?
>
> **Derek:** One moment, please. (*Hold music: 'The Horses', Daryl Braithwaite.*)
>
> **Derek:** The system is allowing me to waive your annual fee, and I can cut your rate to 9.95 per cent, effective immediately.
>
> **You:** Thank you, Derek. Bye-bye.

Huh?

I know what you're thinking …

Barefoot, why wouldn't I just take the interest-free balance transfer from Citibank for 18 months?

Logically, you should.

However, the reason the banks are able to do something as illogical as give you an 18-month repayment holiday is that they know you'll probably spend more money on the new card (at a crazy interest rate) and that you won't pay it off in time.

That's why I've found that for most people it's better to negotiate a lower rate on your existing cards and pay them off one by one.

Having said this, if you really want to go the balance transfer route, it helps to think of it as Keanu Reeves taking the 'Red Pill': you can only take it once, and it's forever. If you're game, here are the instructions:

- **Make sure you can realistically clear your debts off in under 18 months.**

  Be honest with yourself—can you really pay it off in 18 months? If so, do it. (Now you *could* keep playing balance transfer roulette with yet more banks, but you'll eventually end up getting a reputation as a rate tart and you'll screw your creditworthiness. And you won't have paid off your freaking debt!)

- **Get the best balance transfer deal.**

  These deals change all the time. Google 'balance transfer credit cards' and you'll get the current list (we also keep a list of the best deals at Barefootinvestor.com). You want a card with 18 months' free interest and with no balance transfer rate fees (which can be 1 to 2 per cent of the value of your transferred debt).

- **Cut up the new card when it comes in the mail.**

  This is essential. If you don't, the chances of getting screwed will skyrocket.

Domino 3: Eliminate

It's time for some plastic surgery. Cut up all your credit cards. Take a photo, and post it on the Barefoot Investor Facebook page. Get ready for an avalanche of 'likes'.

Domino 4: Detonate

Now it's time to detonate your debts.

I want you to rearrange your list of debts from smallest to largest, using the table below. (Yes, it's the same table from a few pages ago, but this time you're ranking the debts by size.)

Name of debt	Total amount	Interest rate	Monthly minimum
			Total:

We're not focusing on paying off the debt with the highest interest rate (because you should have already negotiated that one down in Domino 2). Instead, we're focusing on building up your confidence by detonating some debts very quickly.

Now, single out your smallest debt.

It could be a parking fine, or $50 you owe a mate. It could be a credit card. Attack your smallest debt by bumping up the repayments so you can knock it over like a domino as quickly as possible. Focus your attention on knocking this smallest debt over *completely*.

And here's the good part: debt is what I call a 'financial fire', so...

Use your Fire Extinguisher (20 per cent of your take-home pay) to 'hose down' your smallest debt.

Then turn the hose to the next debt, and the next, until they're all put out.

But remember: while it's great to put your spare money (Fire Extinguisher) into paying off your debts fast, always make the minimum repayments on all your debts (such as a monthly payment on your credit card) using your Daily Expenses money. This will keep the annoying letters (and debt collectors) at bay.

Domino 5: Celebrate!

When that smallest debt is paid in full, hold a bill-burning ceremony.

Seriously, I want you to go out to your back yard (with an alcoholic beverage of your choice) and burn the statement with a lighter. Celebrating is really, really important. You need to give yourself a pat on the back for having a small win. That's how you build momentum. You're training your brain to win.

The next day, take your momentum and move on to knocking over your next debt domino.

Keep going till you've knocked them all down.

The simple act of setting up a 'domino' and knocking it down will change not only the way you spend, but the way you live. Trust me on this. By directing all your spare cash towards getting out of debt—by making it as real and as painful as possible, until every last cent has been repaid—you'll develop true character and the behaviour required to become financially free.

Finally, know this ...

The Debt Domino will knock out your debt. But what it's really about is rebuilding your confidence. One of the greatest parts of my career has been watching the life-changing results people get playing Debt Domino. I've seen people pay off as much as $60000 and then go on to buy a home and build an investment portfolio. Life is all about momentum. When you feel in control and have a taste for winning, it'll transform your life.

At which point you say, 'Very motivational. But I'm still in debt, dude!'

My reply is that once you go through the process of lining up your dominoes you're already free.

Being in debt is not the same as having a debt problem.

Once you begin pushing that first domino, you're already in control, and you'll soon be debt free.

Okay, time for another 'menu' to put it all together ...

BAREFOOT DATE NIGHT MENU

Week 5

This is your fifth and final weekly Barefoot Date Night (you'll do them monthly hereafter), and we've saved the best for last. Tonight you're going to get out of debt once and for all. Better yet, you're going to join a new club, where the initiation isn't a secret handshake but posting pics of your 'plastic surgery'...

ENTREE:

Grab a pen and write down your debts from smallest to largest using the table on page 92.

Next, it's time to get your game face on and negotiate. Make the phone call to your bank using the word-for-word scripts on page 93.

MAIN COURSE:

Now it's time for some plastic surgery.

Right there at the table I want you to go ahead and cut up your credit cards.

Then pull out your phone, take a picture of it and post it on the Barefoot Investor Facebook page.

DESSERT:

Pavlova (with passionfruit)

Look, cutting up your credit cards is very un-Australian, so you need to do something dinki-di, and few things are more 'Strayan' than eating a white sugary cake smothered in cream and passionfruit.

The move to monthly Barefoot Date Nights

You rock!

If I were standing next to you, I'd give you a fist bump (like an awkward uncle trying to be cool).

In the five Barefoot Date Nights so far, you've well and truly set yourself up — saving yourself potentially hundreds of thousands of dollars in fees — and you've now got a financial plan that is so simple you can write it on the back of a serviette.

Because you've done all the fiddly setting-up work, from this point on we're going to drop the Barefoot Date Nights back to once a month.

So I want you to put down the book and pick up your phone (or your calendar) and set the monthly reminders. Having it the same night will make a ritual out of it (Liz and I do ours on the first Tuesday of each month).

Think back to the apple tree:

You've now planted it in the ground, and the roots are taking hold.

Your monthly Barefoot Date Night is providing the regular water and sunshine it needs to grow big and strong.

If you want some extra motivation on the power of scheduling your Barefoot Date Night, flick back to page 11 and see what April and her average-income family were able to achieve in 12 months (overseas holiday, share portfolio, $30 000 off the mortgage). April says it best: 'I have never felt as financially secure as I am now ... I feel excited about my future'.

Liz and I still do a monthly date night, even though we've worked our way through all the steps. It's a chance for us to review our spending, look at our goals and discuss whether we're on track. (Okay, and it's also a chance for us to enjoy nice food, drink wine and spend time together without the kids.)

Mother and daughter pay off tens of thousands of dollars in credit card debts!

Lauren Marks, NSW

I found out Mum had six credit cards, with thousands in debt...When she paid off the last one, we both cried.

My first experience with debt was when I turned 18. I got a letter from my bank saying I could have a credit card with a $500 limit, and I thought, 'why not? That will pay for my formal dress.' They kept upping my limit and, before I knew it, it was maxed out.

Two years into uni, I owed $10000. The worst part is I can't even tell you what I spent the money on. I felt so embarrassed that I didn't tell anyone about my secret debt. When I did eventually tell my boyfriend (now husband) he couldn't believe it and helped me take my first steps to facing my debt.

And then I read the *Barefoot Investor*. I got so inspired by it—I transferred my credit card debt to a zero-interest loan for 12 months. In that time, I paid off every last cent. Then I started saving.

My husband and I are now saving a deposit for a home. We have $25000 so far and are aiming for 20 per cent.

Because Barefoot has had such a big impact on my life, I bought a copy of Scott's first book for my mum. She called me and broke down, revealing she had six credit cards, with thousands in debt. She cried and I felt sick.

I told her, 'It's okay, I've read about Scott's Domino Your Debts strategy, you can do this' and I helped her set it up, starting with the smallest debt. Every time she paid one off, we'd celebrate. When she paid off the last one we both cried, because I know that feeling.

Now Mum has started saving the amount she'd been paying off the debt. For the first time in her life, she has 'Mojo'.

And those savings have literally been a lifesaver for Mum, who was diagnosed with thyroid cancer at the beginning of 2016.

If she didn't have savings, she would have had to wait four months to have surgery in the public sector. If it had spread, we would never have forgiven ourselves. Thankfully, with her Mojo she could afford to pay $15000 for the treatment she needed and they got the cancer out within two weeks of diagnosis.

She's now got the all-clear.

Recap of Part 1: Plant

So there you have it.

In three simple Barefoot Steps (and five Barefoot Date Nights) you've achieved what 95 per cent of the population will never do.

You have:

- made a commitment to becoming a little wealthier each day

- set up your financial infrastructure so you'll pay zero bank fees, and, more importantly, put your day-to-day money decisions on autopilot

- rounded up your long-lost super funds into an ultra-low-cost fund (if you ever get to hang out with some finance professors you're going to absolutely *dominate* the personal finance conversation)

- done something very un-Australian by cutting up your credit card(s) and begun the process of domino-ing your debts

- become one of the 7 per cent of Australians who have the right amount of insurance.

And we're just getting started.

Now it's time to grow, baby, grow!

Part 2
GROW

You're about to enter the most exciting part of the book.

You've planted your wealth tree by getting your Serviette Strategy set up, and domino-ed your debts (or started doing so).

Now it's time to grow!

We're going to focus on earning more, saving more, and then intelligently and tax effectively compounding your money over and over.

Let's get cracking!

In 'Grow' I'm going to:

- explain how you can double your income

- show you how to save up a six-figure house deposit in 20 months, and introduce you to a young, single woman on average dough who bought her own home

- step out a simple strategy that puts your investing on autopilot so you'll never have to worry about money again

- secure your kids' financial future—first by explaining my 'jam jar' approach to teaching financial education, and then by giving you an investment plan that could deliver a $140000 cheque on their 21st birthday

- reveal my plan to triple your money in 10 years with a little-known investment property play.

Plus I'm going to show you what Harvard University says is 'the number one purchase for happiness'.

It's time to grow, baby, grow!

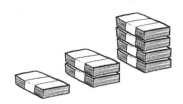

How to double your income

You'll notice with the Serviette Strategy that at the top of the buckets there's a tap—your income. (If you missed it, turn back to Step 2.)

Well, now we're going to turn that tap on full.

It's about showing you how to make more money so that you can fill your buckets faster.

This is a U-turn from most finance books.

Most of them say things like, 'If you cut out your daily latte and invest that money, in 30 years you'll have $165000!'

Uh-huh.

Listen: there's a limit to how much you can save, but there's no limit to how much you can earn.

If you want to drink a latte each day—or for that matter an $80 bottle of plonk that some snotty sommelier describes as having an arresting bouquet of berries, with a hint of…pencil shavings (which in a blind taste test you couldn't pick from an $8 Aldi bottle)—all power to you!

Sniffy-sniff away!

Just make the conscious decision to turn your income tap and let the money gush out into your buckets.

That's what I did.

Many years ago, I walked into the Australian Stock Exchange in a cheap suit. I knew I wanted to do something different…I just had no idea what it would look like.

I didn't have a grand plan.

(No-one does.)

Yet I did have a passion.

I enjoyed teaching people about money and making it fun. Most of the stuff written about finance was as dry as my mouth on a Sunday morning. I'd even come up with a name that captured what I was trying to do: kick off my shoes and tread my own path.

I called it 'The Barefoot Investor'.

Excitedly, I took it to my boss at the ASX—someone older, more experienced and more knowledgeable—to get his feedback.

I had no idea at the time, but this would be the worst—and best—meeting of my life.

You're joking … right?

It was like he pricked me with a pin.

I was like a balloon deflating right there in his office.

Pss…sss…sss…

As I stood in front of my boss, I could literally feel all the air and the life being sucked out of me.

He was brutal:

'The *Barefoot* Investor?' he said in a high-pitched, mocking voice.

Then he leaned back in his chair, put his hands behind his head and showed his sweaty, pit-stained shirt.

'What the hell does that even mean? As in…no shoes?! Haw, Haw, Haw! You're joking…right?' he said, studying my face intently for signs I was pulling his leg.

His smile slowly faded as it dawned on him I wasn't joking.

But I was too deflated to talk, so I just stood there, wheezing.

What a … prick.

A few minutes later I limped away from his office and slumped back inside my cubicle.

'How'd you go?' asked my workmate.

'He basically said it was a dumb idea … oh, and a *really* bad name.'

It was the best of times; it was the worst of times

I needed a second opinion—and the best second opinion always comes from your mum.

'Well I think that sounds like a *lovely* idea,' said Mum.

(To be fair, if I'd told her I intended to be the 'Cabbage Patch Doll Investor', she'd have been on board with that too.)

It was her opinion against that of a stock exchange veteran.

I chose to listen to my mum.

But I didn't up and quit my job like some accounts clerk who makes it to the second round of *The Voice*: 'So long, suckers. I quit! I'm going to be famous!'

What I did do was work my arse off on my idea for the next few years. Specifically:

I worked for free …

While continuing to work full time as a stockbroker, I started a weekly money talkback radio show on university radio station SYN FM.

Then I did some freelance work …

The success of the radio show put me on the radar of some newspaper editors, who offered me freelance writing on the side. It wasn't lucrative—I could have earned more money cleaning toilets at McDonald's—but I preferred helping people with their money than scrubbing their dunnies.

Then I took on more freelance work than I could handle …

The success of my freelance writing led to my first book deal. That sounds kind of Hollywood—like I was a big shot. Truth is, I wasn't even a peashooter. My publisher described our deal as a 'punt' and hoped the book would sell a thousand copies … if we were lucky.

I had other ideas. Each weeknight I stayed back at work and wrote like a man possessed. I remember my girlfriend at the time ringing me one Wednesday around midnight and complaining, 'Why are you still at work? You're a freak!' (We didn't last.)

Then I started my own business full time ...

Five years after that first deflating conversation with my boss, and after hundreds of hours of work (both paid and unpaid), I finally made the transition to working full time at Barefoot. And it felt great.

Okay, that's me. Now let's talk about *you*.

See, as you get older, some people—even well-meaning people—will try and keep you in your box.

I'm going to get you out of that box. So let's talk about your job.

Welcome back to high school

You thought you were done and dusted with high school, didn't you?

Welcome to the workforce.

For many people the place they work looks remarkably like a Year 8 science class.

There are little cliques, each trying to run the show.

There are bullies, who try and make you feel stupid (to mask their own low self-esteem).

There's the teacher (your boss).

And there are hijinks behind the shelter shed (Friday night knock-off drinks).

It's not surprising when you think about it: according to a Gallup poll in 2011, almost two-thirds of Aussie workers consider themselves to be 'emotionally detached' from their employer. They turn up to work, punch the clock and do the bare minimum.

And what do a bunch of bored, frustrated, unengaged Year 8 kids do?

They bitch.

They blame their superiors.

They gossip.

And they feel threatened when anyone looks like they're going to show them up.

Not every workplace is like a Year 8 science class, but the research doesn't lie: the majority of the people you work with are lukewarm about their job.

That's why you'll find some co-workers who'll try to pull you down at every turn, telling you it can't be done, you're too young, too old, too inexperienced. Don't get ahead of yourself, they'll say, like they're looking out for you.

I've worked with a lot of these people. They come in all sexes, ages and management levels—but the one thing they have in common is that they're bitter because they've never done it themselves, and they sure as hell don't want you to either.

Here's the deal, though: you're going to spend 90 000 hours of your life working.

That's a huge chunk of your precious time on earth. Add in sleeping, the daily commute and sitting on the can and there's not much left over. You'll spend more time at work than you do with your family and friends.

School's in. Take notes.

How to earn $5000 in an hour

We've all been in a performance review. Most of us have them once a year.

But how much time did you put into preparing for it?

If you're normal, you spent about 10 minutes thinking about it on your way to work that morning.

Well, I'm going to show you how to make $5000 in an hour. I call it 'Career Compounding' (just like compounding your investments, we're going to compound your salary).

A wealthy old stockbroker once told me something I've never forgotten: 'The difference between being broke and becoming a millionaire is as little as getting a $5000 pay rise a year'.

He's right, so let's get busy.

1. Make a commitment

Sounds a little wishy-washy, right?

A 'commitment'—what does that mean?

If you're going to earn more money than you did last year, you need to do things you've never done.

The simplest way to become a multimillionaire is to commit to being the best. Besides, you're getting out of your PJs, fighting traffic and spending the best part of the day working, so why not be the best at what you do?

Very few people ever make that commitment. Those who do, get paid a disproportionate amount for their 90000 hours. Do you think a CEO works 200 times harder than a regular worker? Of course not. And trust me, they sure as hell are not 200 times smarter.

They're just committed.

2.   Do your homework

One week before your performance review, take out your position description and look at it from your boss's point of view. How does your job make their life easier? How does it contribute to the company? Most jobs can be boiled down to three fundamental tasks. Write them down. Then set yourself an ambitious goal for each task over the next 12 months, and write them down too.

3.   Take control of your performance review

I'm now a boss, and I do performance reviews. Most people turn up unprepared and crap on. They wing it. It's obvious they haven't put any thought into it.

Not you. You may be the one person in the entire organisation who's actually prepared for it. That'll make you stand out.

Present your list of prioritised tasks and goals, and genuinely ask your boss for feedback. You're not doing this to be a brown-noser. You're going to devote time each day to it for the next 12 months, so you want to be crystal clear that you and your boss are on the same page. Take notes on whatever they say and, for God's sake, smile.

4.   Put your goals in your calendar

You now have your ambitious 12-month goals, so put them in your calendar as a daily reminder. The key to progress is doing a little every day, and tracking your progress. You'll be surprised how much you can get done by focusing on your goals rather than bitching about the boss.

5. Casually follow up with your boss over the next 12 months

Notice the word 'casually'. Do not make this weird. Don't be like the desperate guy wanting a second date who can't read social cues. Be like Fonzie. Cool.

You want to frame it in your boss's mind that you're hungry, but humble. Be dependable, ready to take on more responsibility. Then casually show them the progress you're making towards your goals.

The ultimate payoff

So how much time does Career Compounding take?

Probably just a few hours or so a week around your other work—no overtime needed.

How much could it end up making you?

An extra $5000 over the next year (and it only took you an hour's work). And, just like investing, the longer you do it, the better off you'll be. In time, you'll take giant leaps up the corporate ladder. That's how compounding works. So stop for a minute and think about what a difference this could make to your life.

Then shut down Facebook.

And do it.

Please, give me your excuses

When I challenge people to do Career Compounding, there's always someone who tells me it won't work for them. They'll say, 'You don't understand, my boss models himself on Donald Trump' or 'I'm a government employee' or 'I'm a stripper'.

Okay, so let's get practical.

Who are the highest paid people you work with?

Chances are they're no smarter than you, and they may not work much harder than you. What's different is that they'll be doing one of two things: leading people, or 'bringing home the bacon' (providing the goods, marketing the goods or selling the goods).

These two roles will always be in demand, and will always be very well paid. Every organisation—from tin-pot start-ups to mega-multinationals—needs them. That's because they directly affect the business's bottom line.

So if your current position isn't focused on leading people or bringing home the bacon, you have two choices:

First, you can spend some down time on your next Barefoot Date Night thinking about which of these roles would suit you.

(Okay, so if you're currently a receptionist, you can't just bust open the marketing meeting and start presenting your ideas. But you could offer to help the marketing manager by doing some admin for one of their projects outside your normal hours, for free. And while you're helping, you could (a) learn everything you can about the marketing challenges your business faces, and (b) develop a network of people higher up the chain than you. The added bonus is that you make yourself more valuable, and that almost always leads to more money.)

Second, if climbing the corporate ladder is not floating your boat, you should take my lead and turn your passion into profit…

Get a bit on the side — fast

The easiest way to make extra money quickly — as in next week — is to freelance.

Freelancing cuts through the bulldust and allows you to road-test your ideas, your pricing strategy and your skills … all without leaving the security of your day job.

If you've thought about doing your own thing, you're in good company.

A 2016 survey by the NAB found that one in three Aussies wants to be their own boss — and for young people it's one in two.

What can you do?

Well, you can do something related to your work. If you're a teacher, you could become a tutor or a trainer. Or you could try something you're passionate about but have zero experience in, like I did when I started writing for newspapers.

What stops most people from turning their day job into their dream job is they don't feel they have any contacts. It makes sense. That chestnut 'it's not what you know, it's who you know' is true.

Well, when I started out I had zero contacts. As in none. No-one knew who I was. I was a kid from the country who looked more like a boyband member than a stockbroker.

Yet I didn't dwell on it.

Instead, I told myself a different story. I said, 'I'm going to hustle and make my own freaking contacts'.

And that's what I did.

And that's what every successful person who started from scratch has done.

And if you're going to win, that's what you're going to have to do too.

Making connections is easier than you think. I found that people respected me more because I'd come from nowhere and they could see I was fighting my way up.

When I started out I wrote down the names of three people I wanted to meet and work with over the following 12 months. Then I worked along until I got to meet them. How? I just thought of ways to reach out and help them in some way, for free.

I learned this from Eddie McGuire. People say he's a super networker, but that's selling him short. The Eddie I know is one of the most giving people I've met. The bloke is forever doing charity nights and helping people out. He pays it forward.

Using that same technique, I scored an interview with Sir Richard Branson on my community radio show. I rang his secretary and gave her my pitch: I had a youth-focused audience that Branson could connect with (and I told her we'd have lots of fun). He came on the show, had a great time, and even offered to endorse my first book. Years later I helped him launch Virgin Money in Australia.

Swing on the trapeze

Now, some people will compound their career by either climbing the ladder or 'bringing home the bacon'.

Others are happy to get a bit on the side and earn some extra coin. If you start your business off part time, you may work out that what you've really got is a great part-time gig that can domino your debts or build a huge investment portfolio. What's so bad about that?

Then there's people like me, who enjoy their side business so much that they make it their life's work.

If this is you, awesome. But I advise you follow a strategy I call 'swinging on the trapeze'.

And it's this: don't let go of the swinging bar (your secure pay cheque) until you're safely holding the next pay cheque (from your successful business).

Let me show you how *not* to swing from the trapeze.

Colin works in Accounts at his local shire office. He wants something more in life, so he abruptly quits his job to start his own event planning business.

Here's what that looks like:

With a copy of *How to Start a Lifestyle Business in 4 Steps*, Colin jumps off the ledge without a safety net.

'I can't even see the trapeze bar, but I'm jumping anyway: I've never felt more alive!'

The crowd hold their breath. Guess what happens next?

Splat!

When I started the Barefoot Investor I made sure I didn't jump till I was ready.

For years I worked 80-hour weeks, combining full-time, freelance and unpaid work. If you're not willing to do that for at least the first 12 months, there's a good chance that—like Colin—what you're really doing is running away from a job you don't like.

If you can't handle very, very hard work, you're probably not cut out for running your own business.

How you can double your income

By this time you might be thinking, 'Well of course this all works in the swashbuckling world of high finance, but what about for someone in an average job…and where does the "double your income" bit come in?'

I see you, and I raise you. Let's take a look at the most boring man in the world, with the most boring job in the world—my editor.

['Get stuffed!'—Ed.]

When I wrote my first book, they assigned me an editor by the name of Wally.

That was more than a decade ago.

He'd been working in the publishing salt mines, earning a princely $27 000 a year.

'That's not enough. You could be earning $200 000 a year,' I said.

He looked at me like I'd just asked him about his prostate.

'Whaaattt? You just can't earn that money in my industry…have you seen what's happening to bookstores?' he replied.

Wally was about to swing on the trapeze.

On my instruction, he began to take on more freelance gigs.

One job brought him another, and then another. After about six months, he had seven or eight going at one time (including mine), all while continuing his day job.

After a year of hard yakka, he sat down with his wife, and together they decided that he should go full-time freelance.

By this time he hadn't just doubled his salary, he'd tripled it.

Fast forward to today and Wally does a mix of contract work, freelancing and teaching on the side—and my prediction proved right. He now earns more than $200 000 a year. (How's that for 'doubling' your income!)

If he can do it, why not you?

Prove them wrong

A few years ago, I happened to be in the same restaurant as my old manager from the stock exchange.

He acted like he didn't see me.

But I know he did.

Since the time he'd attempted to deflate my balloon, I'd pumped myself up again.

I've compounded my career, swung on the trapeze—and had a ball doing it.

And I've proved them all wrong.

All the people who wanted to see me fail.

All the people who told me that I couldn't do it.

All the people who laughed at me and my idea.

Every single one of them.

And you will too.

At any stage of the game—regardless of your educational level, upbringing or age—you can decide to leapfrog the pettiness of people to achieve your goals. When you make a commitment and have the courage to stick with it through thick and thin, you'll double your income—and more.

Over to you.

STEP 4
BUY YOUR HOME

You can use your buckets to save up a deposit—fast!

I still believe in the Great Australian Dream of owning your own home.

However, I've also seen the dream become a nightmare for many first home buyers, who catch Hills Hoist envy and take on too much debt.

So next we'll cover the practical realities of making the biggest purchase of your life:

- Should you wait for the housing market to crash before you buy?
- Should you buy an investment property first?
- Is rent money really dead money?

And I'll lay out a commonsense plan that could see you in your very own home in as little as 20 months.

Plus, we'll meet a young woman who did it all on her own.

How to buy your home in 20 months

The first time I ever spoke to my wife—then a single 20-something TV producer at *The 7PM Project*—she casually explained that she lived in an inner-city one-bedder.

I assumed she rented.

I was wrong.

Then I asked if she'd bought it with her ex-boyfriend.

Nope.

Then I hinted she must have wealthy parents.

Bump-bow.

Hold up, dear reader, I have to call time out for the next paragraph.

See, as I write this, our sons are still reading Golden Books. But one day they'll read these words. So boys, here's a life lesson from me to you: *Daddy was acting like a chauvinist pig, and Mummy was a smart young woman who didn't need a man for her financial plan.*

Alright, let's get back into it.

On one of our first dates, Liz cooked me dinner using a stove she'd found abandoned on the footpath. Her brother had picked it up, spruced it up and installed it. After she told me about her 'find', I proceeded to eat my roast chicken very slowly. Frankly, I was a little worried that a homeless dude may have found it first and used it as his ensuite. 'Obviously, I scrubbed it clean, Scott', she scolded (for the first, but certainly not the last, time).

For the rest of the evening we sat romantically on cushions, because there was only one chair (and we weren't that friendly yet), and I spent the evening admiring her DIY paintwork.

It wasn't a place I would have bought—it was far too small and, as an investor, I've seen people get screwed investing in shoeboxes like this. Yet the point is that my wife bought her place as a home first and an investment second. It had a car spot, a refurbished oven and a little brick bookcase—and most importantly, it was all hers.

Look, I'm a finance guy, so I can't lie...I was totally turned on by the fact that Liz had bought her home, given that property is so expensive. No smokey eye-shadow needed to get old Barefoot's juices flowing—just show me those mortgage papers, baby. Oh-my-God, that's so...hot!

Yes, housing is ridiculously expensive

Australians are nutty about property: we speak about it, watch lame TV shows about it (one of which I've hosted) and borrow heaps of money to attain it.

Australia has one of the highest levels of home ownership in the world. Interestingly, in many European countries home ownership doesn't have the same attraction, mainly because they have decades-long leases.

If I were a philosopher—which clearly I'm not—I'd suggest it all comes back to our convict history of trying to establish our roots and live the Australian dream. But I'm more of a convict than a philosopher, so I'll stick with the facts:

- Australia has some of the most overvalued property in the world.
- Australia has the highest levels of household debt in the world.
- Australia has the lowest interest rates in history, so repaying that debt is (kind of) manageable today.

Join the dots.

Look, I own property, but I certainly haven't drunk the Kool-Aid. The truth is that housing in most parts of the country is ridiculously expensive. *The Economist* magazine has labelled the Aussie housing market the biggest financial bubble in history.

And yet, regardless of what prices do in the short term, I still passionately believe that owning your own home is one of the best financial decisions you'll make.

Why?

Well, owning your own home is like a 30-year forced savings plan — and any gains you make over that period are tax free. Yet buying a home isn't just a financial decision, it's an emotional one. After all, it's where you'll raise your family. It's your castle. The day I bought my first place was one of the proudest moments of my life. It'll be the same for you.

> **Here's you:** Thanks for the motivational *rah*, Barefoot. But house prices are so ridiculously expensive. With the amount of money I earn, and what I've got saved, I can't even afford a dogbox in Dubbo! At this rate I'll never buy.
>
> **Here's me:** Yes you will.

The real question (without the drama) is *when* will you buy your home?

Is rent money dead money?

Someone, somewhere, has told you this — but they're wrong.

Rent money is *not* dead money.

Well, at least not in the short term while you get your life and finances in order.

What am I getting at?

You don't want to be pushed into making the biggest financial decision of your life.

Too many people are, either out of FOMO (fear of missing out — prices are rising so I have to get in!), or guilt (if we bring our baby home to a rented house … he'll grow up and get a neck tattoo of Miley Cyrus), or pressure (What's wrong with you? Why haven't you bought a home yet?).

Take it from me: buying a home isn't always a sign of financial strength — sometimes it's a sign of financial stupidity. Almost anyone can buy a home with little to no savings, and more often than not they become the financially insecure people I deal with.

Financial stress rips families apart.

Ultimately it's you who has to put your hand in your pocket for decades, so for God's sake own your decision. Look, I'm the guy people contact when everything goes pear-shaped. I've been doing this for years and I see people make the same mistakes over and over again.

Let me share them with you.

Mistake #1: They're waiting for a crash

Ever wondered why news websites publish so many stories about an impending housing crash? It's because it's clickbait to a generation that's priced out of the market and has given up—thinking the only hope for buying is a crash.

That's a cop-out.

You can't plan your life around something you have no control over—the only thing you can control is yourself and your savings. The time to start preparing to seize opportunity is right now.

Which leads me to…

Mistake #2: They buy a home they can't afford

The word 'mortgage' comes from Old French and roughly translates as 'an agreement till death'—and that's exactly what many young families enter into when they mortgage themselves to the hilt.

Things tend to come in threes—I call it the Triple Ms: Marriage, Mortgage, Midgets.

One of my wife's friends came to me for financial advice.

She and her husband were both earning decent dough when they got hitched (marriage). So it didn't seem too much of a stretch to buy their dream home in a leafy suburb of Melbourne (mortgage). What comes after a bird makes its nest?

Midgets. And sleep deprivation. And, later, school fees.

A few years later, she was a stay-at-home mum. Like most people who borrow too much for their dream home, it quickly became a nightmare—and meeting the minimum repayments became a maximum stress.

Is it any wonder the median duration from wedding bells to divorce bills is 12 years?

The truth is that buying a home *creates* financial stress and insecurity—until you get ahead of your mortgage. As all homeowners know, running a home is expensive, costing up to 5 per cent of the purchase price each year.

And this is magnified when you take on more debt than you can afford.

Mistake #3: They buy an investment property first

Here's the pitch young couples give me: 'We'll buy an investment property to start off with, just to get our foot in the door, and use the equity to buy our family home in five years'.

I'm yet to see this plan work (the only exception being couples who buy an investment property to eventually move into). Reason being, the upfront and ongoing costs of owning a home take years to recoup.

We'll discuss buying an investment property in greater depth in Step 5, but for now my advice is simple: if you want a family home, save up and buy one.

Mistake #4: They rent but forget to save

Renting is generally cheaper than owning because you don't have to pay interest or upkeep. So, financially, you'd be better off renting and then investing the difference into the sharemarket, at least according to a research report by none other than the Reserve Bank of Australia.

It makes sense. While some people argue that rent is dead money, so is paying interest to a bank. And over a 30-year mortgage you'll spend more money paying interest to the bank than you paid for the original cost of the house.

And when you add in stamp duty, legal fees, wear and tear and selling costs at the end, you'd be better off renting and investing the difference.

The only problem?

No-one ever saves the difference.

I can work wonders with a spreadsheet and convince you any number of ways you'd be better off, but you don't live life in a spreadsheet. In the real world there are off-spreadsheet factors, one being that as a renter you don't have the security of tenure. And that extra cash can easily be frittered away, especially if you move every 12 months or so.

Mistake #5: They don't consider other options

There are options if you really want to own your own home.

You can move into the city:

A few years back I made a bold prediction that inner-city apartments (especially in the Melbourne CBD) would be selling at fire-sale prices within the next few years. Even as I write this, brand-new off-the-plan apartments are selling at steep losses in many parts of the country as the oversupply of apartments starts to bite.

Or you can move to the country:

That's what we did. Less than an hour's commute from Melbourne, you can purchase a home on a large block for roughly half what it would cost in a run-of-the-mill suburb of Melbourne. It's a lifestyle choice: you'll have less of a mortgage, more involvement with your community and more time to spend with your kids.

Okay, so we've looked at the biggest mistakes first homebuyers make. Now let's look at how to do it right, Barefoot style.

How to save for a deposit

When buying your first home, you should save a 20 per cent deposit.

And, you guessed it: it's time to use the Fire Extinguisher again.

Remember, you already have 20 per cent or so of your pay going into your Fire Extinguisher account, to be used for hosing down 'financial fires', as we saw in Step 2.

In Step 3, you used that Fire Extinguisher to domino your debts.

Now, in Step 4, you're going to use the Fire Extinguisher to save for your house deposit (assuming you've completed Step 3 by domino-ing all your debts, that is).

Why 20 per cent?

Saving a 20 per cent home deposit proves (to yourself, as much as anyone) that you're a good saver. But the main reason is that having a 20 per cent deposit will mean you won't be hit with lenders' mortgage insurance (LMI).

LMI is the bank's insurance against you not being able to make your repayments.

And you pay for it.

And it's very expensive.

If you buy a $500000 home with a 5 per cent deposit, you'll pay LMI of $15722.

It gets worse: because you'll have to tack the LMI onto your loan, it'll end up costing you around $30000 by the time you've paid off your mortgage.

Then it gets even worse: if you switch banks for a better home loan rate, you may well have to pay another $15722.

Remember: this insurance doesn't protect you—it protects the lender.

It's a total waste of money.

Want to get there faster?

First, read 'How to double your income' on page 105 again, and start swinging on that trapeze.

Second, save like crazy. The average full-time pre-tax wage in Australia is $81530, or $5000 a month in the hand (excluding super). So a couple both earning average wages could live off one income (very frugally) and save a $100000 deposit in 20 months.

But hold your horses.

Saving a deposit is like the Socceroos beating Togo to qualify for the World Cup. It's the beginning of the campaign, not the end. In other words, you want your mind to be set on *owning* your home outright, rather than just limping over the line with a deposit.

So don't set up impossible savings targets that you won't be able to sustain in the long run.

Yeah, Nah: First Home Super Saver Scheme

Like a divorced Disneyland dad, the Government has tried to win over young 'uns with the introduction of the First Home Super Saver Scheme in 2017, in an effort to 'tackle' housing affordability.

No, seriously.

Here are the basics:

You can divert extra money into your super ($15 000 max per year), then draw it out as a deposit on your first home. The maximum you can save is $30 000 per person ($60 000 a couple).

Why do it?

Because you'll pay less tax ... and paying less tax equals more deposit.

Let's take the case of Mandy: she earns $65 000 as a professional wrestler and is saving for a deposit on her very own wrestling ring. At her top rate, Mandy pays 32.5 cents in the dollar in tax, plus the Medicare levy. So she could earn $10 000 and be left with just $6550. However, if she put that $10 000 into super (15 per cent flat tax rate), she'd have $8500.

No-brainer, right?

Then when she's ready to buy her first home, she'll be hit with an exit tax (set at 30 per cent below her marginal rate) when she takes her deposit savings out of her super.

If your eyes just glazed over, that's okay.

Here's the guts of it: after three years of using the First Home Super Saver Scheme, Mandy will have $25 833 for a deposit—$6314 *more* than if she'd saved via a standard bank account.

So, let's get to the point: should you open one up?

Yeah ...

You could consider opening a First Home Super Saver if you're planning on buying a home in the next few years, and you already have a decent deposit. After all, it could be worth $12 628 *extra* to an average earning couple (based on Mandy shacking up with The Hulk), compared to saving in the bank.

Nah ...

However, do *not* open a First Home Super Saver if you're not planning on buying a home for up to five years.

(Parents, grandparents—don't open one up for young kids.)

Huh? Isn't Barefoot about the long term?

Yes, but what happens if the Government is voted out and the new mob decide to 'ghost' the First Home Super Saver Accounts (like you did with that mummy's boy you dated twice in 2004)? Well, if the scheme were scrapped, it's possible your savings could be locked up in your super till you retire.

Home is where your heart is

My plan with Liz was as simple as it was romantic: I wanted to get married, move back to the country and live on a sheep farm where our kids could run around, explore and skin their knees. Nothing fancy. No Kardashian lifestyle. Simple. Affordable. Enjoyable. Meaningful.

We could have lived in Toorak, like many of my mates, who are mortgaged up to their Audis. Luckily for us we found our own Toorak—60 clicks away in the bush. It's a place where we are laying down deep generational roots (like an apple tree).

The original farmhouse wasn't flash, but we set about making it our castle, bit by bit. We saved up and added a big deck for our son to play on, curtains to block out the hot summer sun and a $45 bench seat from Bunnings where I'd sit in the sun and read the paper each morning.

A month before the fires came through, I remember sitting on the bench seat and saying to Liz, 'No matter how much money we make in the future, I never want to leave this place—I never want to trade up. This is enough. This is home.'

When you stop competing—stop looking for the next place—you can fully engage with your neighbours and your community.

But many people don't seem to want this.

A side-effect of living through the world's longest and strongest property boom is that we're trained in the status-hugging art of 'property pawn'. A house is just a chess piece to hold onto long enough for the equity to rise—then you trade up to a newer, flashier suburb with newer, flashier neighbours.

I've been to homes of friends who live in trophy suburbs with swanky designer-styled interiors. They have 'alfresco areas' (whatever they are) in Melbourne!

The result is they look like something off *The Block*. You could put another card-board-cut-out family in there and you'd never know the difference.

Where are the dorky family photos? Where are the books? Where are the kids' height-markers scribbled on the wall in different-coloured pens?

A home should be your refuge, your castle.

A place where you can relax and be yourself—like a comfy old jumper.

The day I bought my home was the proudest day of my financial life—second only to the day I paid the sucker off.

It'll be the same for you too.

Which brings me to…

How we bought our family home

When we were hunting for our family home, we went direct.

What does that mean?

Well, like everyone else, we looked on realestate.com.au, but we didn't stop there.

We also put an ad in our local community newspaper detailing what we were looking for.

We also drove around the area we liked and, when we saw a house we liked, put a short, heartfelt letter in the mailbox explaining that we were a young family looking to buy our 'forever' home. That's using Barefoot Rule 85: 'Don't ask, don't get'.

Hard-arse property people will tell you that emotion doesn't come into buying—or selling—a house. It's a lie. Our little ploy worked and we found our dream property. But here's a confession: I played pricing games with the owner, and we almost lost our forever home.

Learn from my stupidity.

If you find a home that you love and that you can afford, don't play games. Put your best offer in writing, straight off. Let them know you're serious. Get it off the market as quickly as you can. Instruct the real estate agent to present your signed offer to the vendor immediately.

Repeat after me: I will not mess around with my forever home.

A few more tips…

- **Don't believe your bank.**

  A pre-approval for a loan from a bank doesn't mean they'll give it to you. It's a lot like getting a number from an attractive woman at a nightclub. You're a long way from being invited back for coffee—and it may turn out she gave you a wrong number just to blow you off.

- **Don't believe the agent.**

  An agent's job is to drum up as many people for an auction as possible, which is why they under-quote what the property will sell for. Don't fall for it. Instead, do your own research based on recent sales in the local area.

- **An auction is street theatre, and you're the lead actor.**

  I prefer not going to auctions, but sometimes you can't avoid it. So act like you're Donald Trump. Stand next to the auctioneer and eyeball the crowd, and particularly your competitors. Take charge.

  And if the bidding goes over your limit, take your bat and ball and head home—the last thing you want is to go beyond your means. Be strong enough to walk away. There are plenty of fish fingers in the sea.

- **Pay for good legal advice.**

  Make sure you cough up to get good legal advice before you sign anything. An experienced conveyancer is worth their weight in gold.

- **And remember the golden rule of real estate.**

  The golden rule of real estate is not 'location, location, location'—it's 'safety, safety, safety'.

Everything you wanted to know about the biggest purchase of your life — on one page

How much of a deposit do I need?

You need to save up 20 per cent or you'll pay thousands of dollars in lenders' mortgage insurance (LMI).

How much can I afford?

Barefoot Rule 246 states: Always borrow less than the bank will lend you — the repayments should generally be less than 30 per cent of your take-home pay. And if you're planning on having kids in the next five years, factor in the drop in income and the increase in costs.

Should I buy an investment property first?

Not unless you plan on eventually moving into it. It gobbles up your savings and delays you getting into your own home.

Should I wait for the housing market to crash?

No — as long as you've saved up a deposit, and you can afford to buy. If you're planning on living there for at least a decade, don't hesitate; just buy.

Should I buy with friends or family?

Friends? No. How many decade-long share-house relationships do you see?

Family? Possibly. As long as you're planning on living in it for the next 10 years.

Should I get my parents to go guarantor?

No way, José.

What about government grants?

If you're buying a home, you may be eligible for First Home Buyers Grants. Usually your bank will arrange this for you, but to find out more head over to www.firsthome.gov.au

BAREFOOT DATE NIGHT MENU

Buying your home

Let's be honest, saving up a 20 per cent deposit is a huge job for most people. (But it won't kill you, and you will achieve it. I meet people who do it every day). That's why you need to keep the monthly date nights up while you're saving—to keep you on track.

ENTREE:

With the serviette you created on page 75 as your guide, I want you to calculate how many months it'll take you to save up for your deposit. And when you get home, mark it on the fridge, and count it down every month.

Hot dang! You're now way out in front of most people, who prefer to bitch and moan about house prices but never actually put a plan in place.

MAIN COURSE:

Now, over a hamburger and fries, it's time to have 'the talk':

If you're going to get into your first home faster, you've got to get your alpaca attitude going on.

Answer these three questions:

1. How can I drastically cut my rent while I save for a deposit?

   (Think downsizing, moving to a cheaper suburb temporarily, or share housing.)

2. What can I do to earn an extra $10000 (or more) in the next 12 months?

   (Re-read 'How to double your income', and work on your freelancing plans.)

3. How can we live off one wage ... and what would that look like practically?

   Only you can work this one out between you. But believe me, it's good practice for when midgets arrive.

   Your answers to this question will reveal how committed you (and your partner) really are.

DESSERT:

Maybe dessert is something you'll sacrifice in the name of saving up a deposit? Surely not!

I bought my home all on my own!

Danielle Eskinazi, VIC

Now that I'm a homeowner, I've just got this sense of security. As a single woman, that's been life-changing.

Six years ago, I never imagined I would be in a position to buy a house.

I was working in admin, trying to save for a deposit on my own, and getting pretty much nowhere.

I'd spend every weekend looking at places, getting my hopes up, only to have them sell way over my budget. It was completely depressing.

I actually gave up a few years ago. I thought, this is stupid, it's never going to happen, especially given that I was trying to do it on my own.

That was 'pre-Barefoot'.

It was starting to read Scott's emails, and then later joining the Barefoot Blueprint, that things started to turn around for me. I had a plan, and I was determined to make it happen.

First, I set up my buckets and my Mojo account.

Then, I paid off my car. I was out of debt and saving! I started building a share portfolio.

And then the big one.

At the age of 31, I bought my first home!

A three-bedroom townhouse in Melbourne—all on my very own.

I remember putting up the 'Sold' sticker on the board and thinking that I've finally done it! It's actually happened! I've never been more scared, or excited. The first thing I did was put in a doggy door.

Yes, I had to prioritise what was important to me while I saved. But it was worth it.

I made the best decision for me. So many things in life change, but my home doesn't have to anymore, unless I want it to. Now that I'm a homeowner, I've just got this sense of security. As a single woman, that's been life-changing.

STEP 5

INCREASE YOUR SUPER
TO 15 PER CENT

After you've got over the initial shock of buying your home, you're probably wondering what you can do to take things to the next level and really build your wealth. And given you're reading a finance book instead of watching *The Bachelor*, I'm taking it as given that you're ready to play a bigger game.

Well, that's what Step 5 is all about. We're going to put your retirement savings on autopilot by increasing your pre-tax super contributions to 15 per cent (up to your age-based limit). And, we're also going to answer some of the big questions you'll be facing at this time:

- Should I buy an investment property?
- What about building a share portfolio?
- How will I pay the kids' school fees?

To help you work it out, I'm not just going to tell you what I think you should do. I'm going to put my money where my mouth is — and tell you what I'm personally doing with my own money.

Let's get into it.

Your Golden Ticket—becoming an investor

My old man quit school early, like many blokes from the country, and began working at the local servo.

Years later he bought the business and, in doing so, convinced his high-school sweetheart to marry him. He'd always been interested in the sharemarket, and if he were born in another time or place I'm sure he would have loved to have gone to uni and study finance.

Yet he did plant the seeds for my interest in investing.

My life changed the day he sat me down and explained that he'd give me one of his shares in BHP as payment for some odd jobs I'd done: 'You're now an owner of one of the biggest companies in the world... and they'll share their profits with you'. As a kid living in a country town, that rocked my world.

Without either him or me knowing it, that moment changed the course of my life.

Paul Kelly was right: from little things, big things grow.

Let's talk about investing.

Specifically, let's talk about how you can mix the magic of compound interest with the most powerful wealth engine in the history of the world: the sharemarket.

That's the Golden Ticket to never having to worry about money again.

But you know what?

I guarantee you that at least one of your family or friends will warn you that 'the stock market is risky'.

Understand that when it comes to the subject of the stock market, most people are the financial equivalent of Pauline Hanson—they react emotionally out of fear, not facts.

Here's how a typical conversation will go down.

Pauline: Are you really investing in the sharemarket? Are you crazy? It's like a giant casino. It's way too risky. You could lose all your money!

You: Well, if I'd invested $10 000 in a broad-based Aussie share fund in 1970—and left it there—today it would've grown to $1 647 850. On top of that, each year I'd be getting a $68 715 dividend cheque in the mail. That's over six times what I put in at the start, *and* my portfolio would be worth over 1.6 million bucks.

Pauline: That's in the past. There's a huge crash coming. The world is going to hell in a halal basket.

You (theatrically counting with your hands, while you wobble your head from side to side): You want hell? I'll give you hell. Over the past 128 years we've had:

- the First World War
- the Great Depression
- a global flu pandemic that infected 500 million people and killed 100 million people
- the Second World War
- multiple recessions...

(You draw breath, and change hands.)

- the Korean War

- the Vietnam War

- the Gulf Wars

- the 1987 stock market crash

- the Asian financial crisis…

(You change hands again.)

- the Tech Wreck

- the 9/11 terrorist attacks

- the Asian tsunami, which killed 230 000 people

- the Global Financial Crisis (GFC)

- Brexit and, of course, Trumpit.

Sounds like a terrible time to invest, right?

Well, it wasn't. Over that time, if you'd invested a single dollar—$1—in the Aussie sharemarket, it would be worth a staggering $2 037 082 today.

The lesson we can learn from history is that bad stuff happens—look who we elect into Parliament!—but the best days are still ahead of us. More importantly, it teaches us that investing in businesses and holding shares for the long term is how you get incredibly rich.

Pauline: I still think shares are risky.

You: Pauline, the biggest risk is *not* owning shares. I need my shares to keep ahead of inflation when I get older. If I live another 50 years, a loaf of bread will cost $10!

Pauline: But what if you invest in the wrong company?

You: Warren Buffett, the world's greatest investor, is leaving his wife her entire inheritance in a simple index fund that automatically buys the 500 largest companies in America. We're talking about companies like Apple, Google, Facebook, McDonald's, Amazon and Nike. My super does the same thing, but it's also got the 200 biggest Aussie companies—like the banks, Telstra and BHP.

Pauline: Well, I just don't understand shares.

You: Honestly, I don't know a balance sheet from a bedsheet, but I have faith that the world has amazing businesspeople like Facebook's Mark Zuckerberg and Amazon's Jeff Bezos. With my super I automatically become a part-owner in their businesses, and they share their profits with me.

Pauline: I don't like it.

You: Well, I have my plan on autopilot so I don't have to think about it. It just ticks over until the day I retire (and beyond). It's been created with an accurate understanding of historical rates of return, and it's designed to outpace inflation and ensure I'll never run out of money. And it cuts my tax bill in *half*.

That's my plan ... what's *yours?*

Pauline: Please *explain!*

Leave your emotions at the door

Making knee-jerk decisions because you're scared may get you elected to the Australian Parliament (twice), but it'll screw you over on the sharemarket.

When it comes to investing, what matters most is how you behave.

Psychologists explain that our fear of losing money is much stronger than our hope for gain. So, when the market has one of its (totally normal) temporary declines, our fear instinct kicks in and we go all cray-cray, and not in a good way.

Now, I know what you're thinking: 'Mate, that won't happen to me. I'm a totally rational person. I understand the sharemarket over the long term always goes up so it's a case of ... *What's that? The sharemarket is crashing?! Why? Brexit? But I thought Brexit was a washing detergent!? Hang on. Everyone just calm down. I'll just bring up my online broking account. Okay, and here it is ... OMG! OMG! OMG! Sell! Sell! Sell!'*

This chart from one of the world's biggest fund managers, BlackRock, nails how most investors behave.

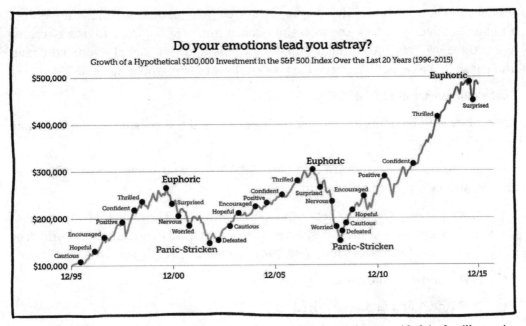

Do your emotions lead you astray?
Growth of a Hypothetical $100,000 Investment in the S&P 500 Index Over the Last 20 Years (1996-2015)

Sources: BlackRock; Informa Investment Solutions. The information provided is for illustrative purposes only.

Thankfully, everything on Wall Street is studied and tracked—even investor stupidity.

Respected US financial research firm Dalbar has been tracking investors' real returns for decades.

And here's the shocker: their research shows that the average investor earned 3.7 per cent annually over the past 30 years, during a period in which a basic index fund returned 11.1 per cent annually. In other words, the average investor *underperformed* the market by approximately 7.4 per cent each year for three decades.

Here's another way to explain it:

Let's say you invested $100 000 in a no-brainer index fund (that automatically buys all the companies that make up a sharemarket index, and tracks the market), and then headed off to the Thai island of Ko Pha Ngan and did nothing but drink buckets of whisky on the beach for the next 30 years. When you return, your $100 000 investment would be worth $2 351 916.

On the other hand, if you'd diligently read the *Wall Street Journal* each morning—hired a financial advisor to pick the latest hot share funds; spent your nights stressing about the 1987 crash, the Asian Financial Crisis and the Global Financial Crisis; and basically behaved like everyone else—30 years later you'd have…$297 415.

That's a difference of $2 054 501.

Bucket-boy won by doing absolutely nothing. He read the gossip pages rather than the business pages.

Even better, he can now retire and earn $100 000 a year—every year—from his shares, and he'll never run out of money.

Remember, I'm not plucking these figures out of the air. The Dalbar study is one of the longest running and most respected research pieces in the finance world. The study found that there were four years when investors really screwed things up:

- 1987 (the stock market crash)
- 1997 (the Asian financial crisis)
- 2000 (the Tech Wreck)
- 2008 (the Global Financial Crisis).

In other words, the damage is done when people check their accounts and go 'Sell! Sell! Sell!' the minute there's a downturn.

So, is a crash coming?

Yes, sooner or later. But the world will not end.

Just remember…throughout history the sharemarket has never, ever failed to move higher.

The Boxing Day sales

Instead of stressing about some crash that may or may not happen, there's a simple way to beat the majority of investors. Shut down your human emotions of greed and fear, and compound your wealth: put your investing program on autopilot.

And you're already doing this with your super. Four times a year your boss posts a cheque to your super fund for an amount that represents 9.5 per cent of your wages. Your super fund then automatically invests it, no matter what the sharemarket is doing.

When the market's going gangbusters and prices are high, your cheque will buy you *fewer* shares and when the market is in a slump and prices are low (or in other words, 'On Sale!'), your cheque will buy you *more* shares.

Does this remind you of something?

Perhaps the Boxing Day sales—when you and your Aunty Flo lined up in the cold at 5 am and then slapped that little redhead who got between you and the Thermomix? Boy did you pick up some bargains that day. And it's the same for investing.

Warren Buffett says you should treat your investments like groceries: 'If you go to the supermarket and there's a sale on, and prices are lower—well, if you're smart—you'll stock up and buy more...The stock market is really just a giant supermarket.'

Becoming a business owner

Think about the richest people you know, or know of.

They'll all share one thing in common: they own a business. That's how you get rich.

Now you can sweat over a stove or try and flog Amway to your (former) friends, but it's a helluva lot easier to become a part-owner in a big, successful business by buying their shares on the stock market.

Yes, I'm talking about investing directly and building your own investment portfolio. At the Barefoot Blueprint, my private investment newsletter, there are thousands of people who are doing just that.

Let's meet one.

Cecilia is a 30-something woman who was born into poverty but went on to build a portfolio of some of the most profitable businesses in the world.

This is her story, in her words.

> One of my friends told me about Barefoot and about shares. I started reading the articles and have followed Barefoot ever since. When I finished my studies and got full-time work, I was able to save more and started buying into the sharemarket in 2013.
>
> I love the idea of being a part-owner of a good company.

I started with just one company and now I've got over $100 000 of my savings invested in 12 companies. Pretty good, considering I earn less than $50 000 per year!

I reinvest the dividends where possible. A lot of people are scared of shares, thinking they will lose money. But what I have learned from Barefoot is to be an investor, not a trader.

When I started, I checked the market almost daily and found myself worrying. Now, I only check once in a while and understand it is a long-term investment.

It feels really good to be in control.

Before Cecilia had a six-figure portfolio (and on a $50 000 wage—you go, girl!), she began with one business. If you follow her lead—and the lead of thousands of Barefooters like her—my recommendation for your first investment would be the Australian Foundation Investment Company (AFIC).

AFIC is a business that trades on the stock exchange. Technically it's a listed investment company (LIC). So it's a company, but make no mistake—AFIC is not in the business of baking bread or running banks. AFIC's business is investing in great businesses (that's what LICs do).

AFIC's been around since before the Great Depression, and has a long, glorious history of beating the pants off fancy managed funds like AMP, BT and Colonial.

With one single investment in AFIC (of, say, $2000), you get the safety of pooling your money with thousands of investors—and exposure to some of the country's most outstanding businesses, such as Coca-Cola, Woolworths and the banks.

And here's the kicker: AFIC's fees are around 90 per cent less than the fees of managed funds—and yet AFIC outperforms the majority of these funds. (Kind of strange, isn't it? You pay more for these other funds and get less…that's quite often the way in the financial world.)

And once you've got your toes wet with AFIC, you can start building your portfolio.

My investment newsletter, the Barefoot Blueprint, has helped thousands of people—young, old, rich and poor—successfully begin building and growing their own investment portfolios. The hardest thing about investing is actually *starting*.

But getting started is what it's all about, because, as the table below shows, the longer you invest, the longer your money has to grow through the magic of compound interest (remember: this is when you reinvest your earnings so you earn interest on your interest).

The power of starting (and compound interest)

If you invest ...	... $0 a month	... $100 a month	... $500 a month	... $1000 a month
After 5 years you'll have ...	0	$7,040	$35,200	$70,399
After 10 years you'll have ...	0	$17,384	$86,919	$173,839
After 25 years you'll have ...	0	$87,727	$438,636	$877,271

Based on an 8 per cent return.

But I don't have any money to invest!

Yes, you do.

Your old mate Barefoot's got one last trick for you.

You probably think I'm talking about an SMSF (self-managed super fund), where you can buy any shares you want within your own super. They've become so popular they're now a fashion statement—all the grey nomads in the caravan park have one.

But I'm not.

As I said earlier, ask anyone who's run their own SMSF and they'll tell you it's a pain in the rump due to all the compliance hoops they have to jump through.

I'd go as far as saying that, unless you're a small business owner wanting to transfer business property assets into a tax-sheltered environment, you shouldn't bother with an SMSF.

Thankfully, there's a cheaper, smarter and much less annoying way to go.

Like what?

Introducing the thinking person's SMSF

It's a thing I call 'SMSF Lite'. It's got the best of an SMSF (you choose how to invest your money in shares) and the best of a traditional fund (low compliance costs and very little hassle).

Who offers it?

Well, there are a number of industry funds that now provide this type of service, though they each do it a bit differently, and they each have their own name for it ('SMSF Lite' is just my term—they'll often call it their 'direct investment' option).

So contact some industry funds to see if they offer this type of product. When you've narrowed your search, go to each fund's website and investigate further.

Look out for three things: fees, insurance options and investment features. Fees will vary from fund to fund, but they'll start at around $180 a year (compared to paying thousands for an SMSF).

Many people have said to me they love the idea of becoming an investor but don't have the ready cash. With an 'SMSF Lite' you can take that $50000 (or whatever you have) in your super fund and start investing it in shares to really boost your returns.

The SMSF Lite that I use

I have my SMSF Lite with Hostplus (because I'm already invested in their ultra-cheap Indexed Balanced Fund for my super). They call it 'ChoicePlus', and it allows you to invest in any of Australia's biggest 300 companies on the stock exchange, together with a range of term deposits and ETFs ('exchange traded funds'—basically index funds).

To be invested in ChoicePlus, you need a minimum of $10000 to kick things off, and at least $2000 must be kept in one of Hostplus's other investment options. It costs $180 a year, versus thousands for a traditional SMSF from an accountant.

By combining ChoicePlus with the Indexed Balanced Fund, I get the best of both worlds: the cheapest super fund in the country together with the opportunity to pick and choose my own shares!

Important

Let me say this again: Hostplus is not paying me a cent. Nor does any other financial institution I mention. I am fiercely independent. I'm just telling you what I do with my own money. You should do your own research.

So should I buy shares inside (or outside) of super?

I think buying shares within your super, via an 'SMSF Lite', is a great idea, as long as you buy wisely (that's what my Barefoot Blueprint newsletter is about).

And you can certainly buy shares in your own name (like Cecilia) if you like. That is, put some of your after-tax income into buying shares.

But why do this if super gives such good tax breaks (taxing you only 15 per cent compared to your usual tax rate of, say, 37 per cent)? The reason you'd do this is if you're younger and you don't want to lock your money away until you retire, as super requires you to do. Or because you want to invest in companies that your SMSF Lite doesn't buy (these funds usually don't allow you to buy very small companies, for example).

So it's up to you and your personal situation. Personally, I do both.

Everything you wanted to know about investing—in one-and-a-bit pages

How do I buy shares?

Within super (SMSF Lite), you can do it pretty easily online.

To invest outside of super, contact your bank. They'll have a share trading service or they'll refer you to one. Buying and selling shares is simple: think of it as a mix of internet banking and eBay. You can even buy shares over the phone with an operator once you've set up your account. You'll need $2000 to start.

Are shares the same as stocks?

Yep, and they're also called 'equities'. But for simplicity I've used the term 'shares' in this book.

How do I know I own the shares?

You'll get a 'holding statement' in the post. And your holding will be registered with your broker. You can sell your shares and receive the money after two business days, and often for less than $20 a trade (as opposed to property, which can take months to settle, and cost you thousands of dollars).

What are dividends?

Dividends are the profits a business shares with you, usually twice a year. And they come with juicy tax credits. If the company offers a dividend reinvestment plan (DRP) you can, instead of taking the cash, choose to automatically reinvest your dividends. Nice.

When should I buy? When should I sell?

Buy shares when you've got the money. Sell your shares when you need the money (hopefully many decades later). Don't be a trader who watches the stock prices every second of the day.

Should I invest in shares or keep paying off the mortgage?

Honestly, I did both. However, making extra repayments on your mortgage is a guaranteed return.

How do I open up an SMSF Lite?

Contact your existing super fund and ask them if they have a 'direct investment' option (or whatever they call it). If they do, get them to send out their charges and terms and conditions. Your SMSF Lite will link directly to your existing super fund (with the same provider) and you'll be able to buy and sell shares just like in a normal share investing account.

My brother-in-law says I should invest in gold. What do you think?

Your brother-in-law is a weirdo.

While gold has historically been the storehouse of wealth in uncertain times, it's been a crummy investment. Wharton Finance Professor Jeremy Siegel keeps long-term (inflation-adjusted) returns of various asset classes, dating all the way back to 1802. Siegel found that if you invested one US dollar ($1) in gold it would be worth $3.11 today. However, if you'd invested that dollar into the sharemarket in 1802 ... it would be worth $1 064 598. Enough said.

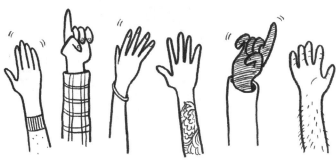

The automatic millionaire—how to put your investing on autopilot

Our family farm is a 50-minute drive from the city (on a good day).

When I was doing the nightly Channel Seven news (the finance, not the weather), I was a road warrior.

'Doesn't it bother you, spending all that time in the car?' people would ask.

'Oh, it's draining … but it's just something I do,' I'd reply, sounding like some duty-bound policeman who risks his life protecting the public—instead of driving to a TV studio, putting on makeup, getting my hair blow-waved and reading an autocue.

The truth?

At home I had a (beautiful but) squawking baby and a (beautiful but) hormonal wife. Spending 50 minutes in air-conditioned comfort with nothing but me, Axl Rose and the open road was as close as I got to 'Paradise City'.

In the beginning, I probably spent an hour or so studying Google Maps to find the quickest route to the studio, and then tested it the next day. Yet once I had the trip down pat, I basically shut off my brain and thought about other stuff.

Honestly, sometimes I'd get in the car, put the key in the ignition, and the next thing I knew I was opening the front door and being greeted by Liz with outstretched arms...handing me our screaming baby:

'Your turn'.

I'm sure you've had similar experiences—you do something so many times (like the daily commute) that you can repeat it without thinking. It becomes automatic.

We're going to do a little bit of work getting your investing program sorted. We're going to work out how much you need to squirrel away to secure your retirement; then we'll put the entire plan on autopilot so you can forget about it and never have to worry again.

Little blue biros

Do you know who reads printed newspapers these days?

Old people.

And as a result of writing a nationally syndicated column for over a decade, in some parts I'm as popular as Ray Martin at a retirement home.

Yet it also means that most weeks I get snail mail from them.

They write in old-school cursive script, inked in blue biro...and they make my heart sink. They're old, they're frail and they're scared.

Some of them sit in their homes with blankets over their legs, frightened of maxing out their power bill.

But don't we live in the richest country in the world?

Yes, global bank HSBC has crowned Australia as having the richest people on the planet—but it's a different story for millions of retirees.

One in three Australian retirees lives in poverty, a global study in 2015 by the OECD found. Australia's high cost of living, together with the fact that our government spends substantially less than the OECD average on pensions, has resulted in millions of older Australians living in poverty.

Another study by HSBC spanning more than 16 000 people in 15 countries found that, on average, Australians run out of their savings 13 years before they die...one of the worst results in the world.

That's the brutal truth I confront each time I open one of those handwritten letters.

When you get to those last 13 years of your life…it's too late to do anything.

So let's make sure you never get into this position.

Contrary to popular belief, it's not sharemarket crashes that wipe out retirees. It's something much more insidious, and it creeps up without you even knowing.

Let me explain.

Faceplanting on a treadmill

Have a look at the following 'shopping list' and see how prices have increased since the 1970s.

	1970s	1980s	1990s	2000s	2016
Average wage	$7500	$10,400	$23,400	$46,800	$80,000
Milk, 1 litre	$0.30	$0.68	$1.03	$1.40	$1.36
Loaf of bread	$0.24	$0.89	$1.67	$2.30	$2.36
Rump steak, 1kg	$3.24	$7.64	$12.62	$12.50	$22.00
House price, Victoria	$37,000	$75,000	$131,000	$299,000	$685,000
Car, Holden	$2,538	$9,046	$24,587	$28,330	$38,000

Since 1970, the price of a basket of goods and services has increased 11-fold—at an average annual inflation rate of 5.3 per cent, according to the Reserve Bank of Australia.

I've already mentioned inflation in this book a few times, and we all have at least a sketchy idea of what it is. Well, now I'd like to explain so that you 'get it'—and never forget it. Because if you don't understand inflation (and take steps to beat it), you're destined to be one of those frail blue biro letter-writers.

Here we go.

Think of inflation as a treadmill chugging along at level '3'.

If you step on the treadmill, you have to walk fast enough to at least match the current speed, right?

What if you just stand still?

You'll do a giant faceplant.

Inflation is like a moving treadmill. Prices don't stand still—they keep increasing year on year (5.3 per cent per annum over the past 47 years in fact).

If you stick your money under the bed, or in a transaction account earning 0.1 per cent interest per annum, then you're doing the equivalent of standing still on that moving treadmill.

It's not safe. It's incredibly risky and it will have a devastating impact on your retirement.

The final quarter of your grand final

How old will you be when you croak?

I asked you this question in Part I—Plant—but if you didn't answer it then, do it now.

Once you have your (admittedly rubbery) figure, subtract your current age.

That's how much time you've got left on the planet: that's what you're preparing for.

Armed with your 'how-many-years-till-I-croak' figure, I want you to look at the new 'shopping list' below and pick the decade you're likely to die in. (So I don't completely freak you out, I've used a conservative 3 per cent inflation, not the historical 5.5 per cent.)

The future is going to be expensive

	2026	2036	2046	2056	2066	2076
Average wage	$107,513	$144,489	$194,181	$260,963	$350,712	$471,328
Milk, 1 litre	$1.83	$2.46	$3.30	$4.40	$5.96	$8.01
Loaf of bread	$3.17	$4.26	$5.73	$7.70	$10.35	$13.90
Rump steak, 1kg	$29.57	$39.73	$53.40	$71.76	$96.45	$129.62
House price, Victoria	$920,583	$1,237,186	$1,662,675	$2,234,496	$3,002,976	$4,035,748
Car, Holden	$51,741	$69,535	$93,450	$125,588	$168,780	$226,827

Assumes 3 per cent per annum inflation.

If you're currently 40 and think you'll live till 90, look at the 2066 figures.

You'll be paying $100 for a steak and $10 for a loaf of bread!

How will you pay for it if you retired at 60 and haven't been paid a wage for 30 years?

Let's return to the treadmill analogy.

Picture yourself at 90 painfully shuffling on that treadmill, gasping for breath, falling over and bloodying your nose. (If you can't picture yourself at 90, picture your parents or grandparents.)

And now for the solution ...

Over the long term the sharemarket has never failed to outpace the rise of inflation.

If you have your long-term savings in growth assets like shares, you'll have enough energy to run at level '8' for the rest of your life, well above the level '3' of inflation.

This is why we invest.

Okay, so you could get 'lucky' and die early, and step off the treadmill of life. But I wouldn't count on it. There's a 50 per cent chance you'll be blowing out 90 birthday candles, according to the NAB.

(And my youngest son, who was born in 2015, will probably reach 100. At which time he'll upload his personality to iTunes and download a new, fully automated body from Tesla. Then he'll be right for another 1000 years—as long as he keeps his iTunes account topped up.)

Anyway, the future is going to be expensive—and the way we pay for it is by investing. And the best place to invest your money for the long term, regardless of your age, is super.

> **Here's you:** Dude, I already have super—my employer pays it.

> **Here's me** (*as I casually eat a mandarin, throw it on the ground, get right up in your grill and scream …*): BUT IT'S NOT ENOUGH! (*Little pips and bits of citrus hit your face, and you recoil in disgust.*)

Yes, it's true, your boss puts 9.5 per cent of your wage into super. But you are being set up to fail (though not if you follow the Barefoot Steps, of course).

So, with your home deposit saved and your home bought, it's time to give your super contributions a boost.

How much? Read on.

Never worry about money again—boosting your super to 15 per cent

Yes, I want you to put 15 per cent of your *gross* wage (that is, pre-tax) into super. (The official term for making pre-tax contributions is 'salary sacrifice', but that phrase just makes me think of Elton John.)

Remember, your employer is already chipping in 9.5 per cent, so you only need to bump it up by a further 5.5 per cent to reach 15 per cent in total.

> **Here's you:** Hang on, I'm a bit freaked out by the whole treadmill thing. Shouldn't I put in more than 15 per cent?

> **Here's me:** Patience, grasshopper. Right now you're going to need the extra money to get through the rest of the Barefoot Steps. And remember, super is locked up until bad things happen—like getting old.

Here's you: Good point! Should I put in less?

Here's me: No! I do not want you to write me a letter one day with a little blue biro. You'll ruin my day.

For you guys at the front of the class, here's some additional reading: the UK Office for National Statistics released a 595-page report that you're not going to read—so I'll summarise it in one sentence: from now on, you need to save 15 per cent of your income to avoid dumpster dining in retirement.

And there's a nice bonus, you'll pay less tax.

Tax cuts!

The government understands that the future is going to be expensive—that's why they bribe you with tax cuts. If you're earning $80000 a year, you can slash your marginal tax rate by more than half by diverting money to super!

Let's do that one more time for the Twitter crowd:

> Money in super = less tax = $$$ in retirement

That's why super should be the centrepiece of your long-term investment program, and why it's the ultimate way to automatically build your wealth.

No willpower needed

Why am I so obsessed with making it automatic?

Because I have as much willpower as a daddy ram in a paddock full of ewes. Yes, I've sat where you are right now. And there are a dozen compelling reasons why you won't get around to doing this.

I get it.

But this is the one thing that your future self will high-five you for.

Look, I'm a little freaky when it comes to talking about super.

I'm like your mate who's just discovered the paleo diet and can't shut up about it: 'Dude, I ate the leg of a goat on Friday and it was so freakin' awesome. *I've seriously never felt this good before!* Here, put down that beer and have some of my bone broth, bro.'

I'm not really like that. Well, maybe a little. But it's with good reason.

Anyway, here's a teacher to give you a final lesson before recess:

Jane is 30, single and a primary school teacher. She earns $72000 a year and has $50000 in super.

She reads this book (which is a bit hard because she's already in it—this book has more random segues than Harry Potter and the Magical Undies) and decides to put her investing on autopilot, boosting her super to 15 per cent, which works out to be an additional $330 per month.

Assuming 8 per cent growth, and 2 per cent inflation, guess how much more Jane has when she retires at 67?

$569073

Even better, she'll retire a double *miyonaire!*

(She's on track to retire with $2063179 in super.)

And she'll pick up a handy tax deduction every year she does it. Way to go, Jane.

Automatic millionaire super scripts

Call your super fund and use the following scripts.

To boost your super to 15 per cent ('salary sacrifice')

> **You:** Could you please email me your standard salary sacrifice form.

> **Super rep:** Have you checked that your employer will allow you to salary sacrifice?

You: Yes, I have. But I also understand that anyone under the age of 75 (who satisfies the work test) can claim a tax deduction for personal super contributions.

Super rep: We've got a live one on the line!

You: So what do I have to do?

Super rep: Just fill out the form I'll email you, and write down that you'd like to salary sacrifice an additional 5.5 per cent of your gross salary, on top of the employer contribution, and then give it to your employer. That'll bring your total to 15 per cent.

You: Anything else?

Super rep: Yes, keep a copy for your records.

If you're self-employed

You: I know I'm not legally required to pay myself super, but I like a good tax dodge. So I'd like to set up a quarterly payment into my super account of 15 per cent of my gross income up to my age-based, pre-tax limit.

Super rep: Okay, here's our BSB and account number to make the transfer.

You: That's it?

Super rep: Were you expecting a parade, and balloons to fall from the sky, sir?

If you're earning under $51 813 per annum ('co-contribution')

You: I'd like to make an after-tax co-contribution towards my super.

Super rep: Smart move. The government will pay up to 50 cents for every dollar you put in after tax, up to certain thresholds.

You: I'm a stay-at-home mum and work three days a week as a bear-catcher, earning $37 000 a year. Please calculate how much I should put into super to get the most from the government.

Super rep: If you make an after-tax contribution of $935, the government will give you an extra $467.

You: I just made a 50 per cent return! When will I get the money?

Super rep: The government will pay your super fund within 60 days of you lodging your tax return.

You: Well, I better ring Old Stubby Fingers my accountant!

BAREFOOT DATE NIGHT MENU

Boost your super to 15 per cent

My 15 per cent super strategy is time-tested. It's totally tax-efficient. And it works. Once you do it, you'll forget about it. After a few months, you won't even notice it. Only problem is that most people never actually get around to doing it.

That's why you're going to make it the centrepiece of this monthly Barefoot Date Night (and to be clear, save this menu for when you're up to Step 5, *after* you've bought your home).

ENTREE:

Whip out your phone and call your fund, using the scripts from page 158.

MAIN COURSE:

Next, fill out the forms to salary sacrifice an additional 5.5 per cent of your gross wage (making a total of 15 per cent), directly into your super fund, and then email it to your payroll officer. If your fund doesn't have a form, you can simply email your boss and ask them to set up the additional pre-tax 5.5 per cent payment on your behalf. It's really simple.

DESSERT:

Even though I don't have a sweet tooth, I never pass on a dessert on Barefoot Date Night. Reason being, I want my brain to become conditioned to celebrating when I score a win (and nothing says 'well done!' like consuming 4000 calories). Or at least that's my justification, and I'm sticking to it.

Up next I've got another way to make you feel all warm and fuzzy.

Stop for a minute and think about how different your life would be if someone had given you this book when you were in your final year of high school.

The truth is, if you've made it this far, you now know more than most people about investing.

Should I buy an investment property?

You want to get ahead.

I get it.

That's why you're reading a finance book and not *Fifty Shades of Grey*.

You're probably starting to earn some bucks, and naturally you want to translate that into a serious return on your money.

And, given that you've always lived in a property, you understand it. So it would be un-Australian not to at least think about an investment property.

So let's talk about whether you should jump in.

But first a disclaimer.

I love property.

I own commercial property, agricultural property, inner-city property and my own home.

But do you know what I love even more than property?

Maths.

You've probably heard so-called experts say, 'Property doubles every seven to 10 years'.

Well, let's run my trusty Casio over that well-worn claim.

On my youngest son's first birthday, the median value of a Melbourne home was $740 995.

That's for your garden-variety metro home (the median price for an inner-city pad was in fact $1.27 million, but for this experiment let's stick with an average metro Melbourne home).

If property doubles every seven to 10 years, let's see how much my son will have to shell out for his own place when he gets older:

By the time he's in primary school, an average Melbourne home will be selling for $1.5 million.

By the time he's in high school, it will be $3 million.

By the time his 22nd birthday rolls around, it will be $6 million.

By the time he finds the love of his life and settles down at 36, it will be a cool $24 million.

And you think housing affordability is tough now!

Poor old mate and his fiancée will have to stump up a $4.8 million deposit!

But it's not all bad. By the time my son retires at 64, it will be worth $384 million, and if he hangs on till his 70s it will be worth $768 million!

Okay, the fact that I've ended the last three lines with exclamation marks is a giveaway that I believe the 'doubles every seven to 10 years' line is rubbish when it comes to property.

Let's talk to a real expert, Professor Nigel Stapledon from UNSW, who researched long-term Aussie property prices for his PhD. The professor found that the average return on Melbourne property from 1901 to 2015 was 2.1 per cent per year, after factoring in inflation.

But wait, there's more: that 2.1 per cent *doesn't* include the money spent on paying interest to the bank, or renovations done on the home.

Professor Robert Shiller, of Yale University, looked at long-term US property prices from 1890 to 2004 and found that inflation-adjusted house prices increased by a miniscule 0.4 per cent annually.

And just to round out the Western world, Professor Piet Eichholtz of Maastricht University looked at property prices in Europe, specifically on one of Amsterdam's most significant canals, Herengracht. He was able to track the buys and sells of a single property for a full 345 years.

The result?

A return of 0.2 per cent per annum after inflation. Real home prices did roughly double, but they took nearly 350 years to do so, says Shiller.

Now it's true that, in some areas in Australia, property *has* doubled every seven to 10 years over the past 24 years—but not when you factor in inflation, interest costs, upkeep and maintenance.

What's more, these figures only show the sale price, not the money spent building or renovating. Say I buy a house for $500000, demolish it and spend $1 million building a new home. I later sell it for $1.5 million. How much have I made? Zero. Yet the house price data reports that the price has gone up 200 per cent.

When you look at the past 24 years from a historical view, this period has been an outlier—a once-in-a-lifetime boom—brought on by some unique factors:

- mortgage interest rates falling from a peak of 18 per cent in the late 80s to around 4 per cent today

- household debt ballooning to 175 per cent of household income, the highest in the world

- tax breaks for negatively geared properties, which have encouraged Baby Boomers to borrow on the equity in their homes to buy loss-making investments.

Hardcore, huh?

Don't put down this book!

People have very strong feelings about property. I know that.

And at this point, 50 per cent of you probably agree with me, and 50 per cent probably don't.

And if you're one of the ones who don't, you're probably skimming this while watching *The Bachelor*, thinking 'I was enjoying this book...until now'.

And there's perhaps a 10 per cent chance that what you've just read has made you so angry that your left eye is twitching as you mumble: I made *three hundred grand* on my apartment, Barefoot, so stick your 2.1 per cent up your arse!

Again, I love property. I mean, I've even made buying a home one of the Barefoot Steps.

But I don't for a moment believe there's a goldmine in my back yard.

The reason house prices are at record highs is that we've taken on record debt at a time when interest rates have fallen to record lows.

It's been a wonderful run for the past 24 years, but will it be for the next 24?

Why borrowing to invest kills compound interest

Albert Einstein said that compound interest is the 8th wonder of the world.

What is compound interest?

It's when you reinvest your income so you earn interest on your interest.

When it comes to buying an investment property, the interest you pay on your borrowings reduces—and, in many cases, totally eliminates—your rental income.

Now most property investors don't really care about the cash their property puts in their pockets—in fact, some are more than happy to accept a loss in exchange for a tax deduction (that's called 'negative gearing').

This works in a once-in-a-lifetime boom when house prices continue to rise, but at any other time it's a recipe for disaster.

And yes, you can make the same argument for borrowing to invest in shares as you can for borrowing to invest in property—in both cases, the interest you pay the bank reduces (or eliminates) the amount available to you to reinvest and compound over time.

Therefore, if you can avoid debt and focus on savings, that's the way to go.

Let me level with you … right now I know I sound about as sexy as picturing your parents on their wedding night. You'd probably find it more titillating to read *From 0 to 130 Properties in 3.5 Years* (another Wiley title, actually), but what my book is about—hell, what I'm about—is keeping you and your family safe.

Debt is a four-letter word

The greatest investor in history, Warren Buffett, is cut and dried when it comes to borrowing to invest: 'Stay away from debt. If you're smart you don't need it. If you're dumb you got no business using it.'

He once described debt as like 'driving a car at 100 miles per hour down a hill with no seatbelt...with a dagger taped to the middle of the steering wheel'.

Well, that sure gets to the...er...*guts* of it.

The dude doesn't do debt. In fact he famously keeps $20 *billion* in cash on hand to take advantage of the inevitable opportunities that arise from people getting into trouble from taking on too much debt.

Of course, your brother-in-law may disagree with all this.

That's fine.

Then again, your brother-in-law hasn't achieved a mind-boggling 2 404 748 per cent return over his investing career now has he?

The truth is this:

Debt always makes things more complicated.

Debt always adds more risk.

Debt always adds more stress (whether you admit it or not).

And if you can avoid getting into debt, you should.

A tale of two investors

To show you what I mean, let's look at two investors, Peter and Paula: one who buys shares and the other who buys an investment property.

The share investor

Peter saves up $5000 and invests it into the Australian Foundation Investment Company (that ultra-low-cost share fund I mentioned at the start of this chapter).

While sitting on the can one day, he opens up his CommSec Share Trading app, types in 'AFI' and purchases $5000 worth of AFIC shares.

The fee for the trade (brokerage) is $19, and two days later the money is debited from his bank account.

Two weeks later he receives confirmation in the post, along with a dividend reinvestment plan (DRP) form that allows him to automatically have his dividends (the regular income payments from his shares) reinvested. He ticks 'yes' on the form and sends it back.

That's it for 10 years.

When Peter goes to sell, it'll be another $19 fee, and the money will be in his account in two days.

The property investor

Paula attends a nerve-racking auction where she knocks out other bidders and buys a two-bedroom apartment for $585000.

It'll be a 90-day settlement.

Straight up, Paula pays an additional $30170 in stamp duty, as well as $3074 in transfers and legal fees, and $58500 as a 10 per cent deposit.

She rents out the apartment for $450 a week, for 52 weeks a year, and earns $23400 a year (see box).

Trouble is, her costs—home loan interest, managing agent fees, insurance, accounting, body corporate, rates, maintenance—amount to $31402.

So, in the first year she's lost $5121… and that's after the negative gearing tax break.

Paula's Property Investment

Purchase price: 2-bedroom flat	$585,000
Stamp Duty	$30,170
Transfer and Legals	$3,074
Total cost of unit	$618,244
Paula puts down a $91,744 to cover the 10 per cent deposit, and stamp duty and legals.	
Annual income: $450 per week, for 52 weeks a year:	$23 400 per year
Cost:	
Interest only loan at 4.25%	$22,377 per year
Lenders Mortgage Insurance (annualised)	$1,425 per year
Property management fees	$1,850 per year
Insurance	$600 per year
Accounting	$350 per year
Body corporate	$2,000 per year
Council and water rates	$1,300 per year
Maintenance	$1,500 per year
Total yearly costs	*$31,402 per year*
Total yearly loss	*$5,121 (after the negative gearing benefit)*

*Based on an annual income of $78 832.

Here's Paula's problem.

She's losing money every single year, so the only way she can make money is via capital gains—that is, selling the property for more than she bought it (and then, she'll be hit with capital gains tax, which will push her into a higher tax bracket).

So how much does she need to sell it for in 10 years' time just to break even?

Let's do the figures:

Total annual losses: $51 210

Agent's selling commissions and legals: more than $15 000

Stamp duty, legals: $33 244

So Paula needs to sell her apartment for $100 000 more than she paid for it, just to break even. And that's before taking into account any capital gains tax.

Of course, no-one knows what the next 10 years of returns will bring, but we do know the costs she'll be lumped with along the way.

No doubt if Paula is like most people, she'll gloss over the almost $100 000 in out-of-pocket costs, and she'll only calculate the difference between what she bought it for and what she sold it for!

How to really make money in property

Okay, so I've told you how to lose money in property (or just break even). Now let me tell you how I make money in property.

A few years ago I invested in a property play called the BWP Trust, which trades on the Australian Stock Exchange.

You've probably never heard of it, but I guarantee you've been in one of the buildings it owns. That's because BWP Trust owns 80 Bunnings Warehouse properties (not the businesses themselves … just the big green sheds they're housed in).

At the time I made a bold prediction to my Barefoot Blueprint investment newsletter subscribers: over the next 10 years I would *triple* my money.

Even better, I'd do it without the hassle of buying an investment property.

No bong-smoking renters … the tenant is Bunnings, owned by conglomerate Wesfarmers.

No 12-month lease turnovers … Bunnings signs up for 20-year leases, with options thereafter.

No upkeep costs...it's written into the lease that Bunnings is lumped with *all* upkeep costs.

No dealing with uninspired rental agents...the Trust handles all that for me, and automatically reinvests my rent into buying more.

No worries about banks jacking up my interest rate...because I didn't borrow any money.

No guesswork on my returns...they were based on set yearly rent increases underwritten in ultra-long rental agreements.

And what about my prediction of tripling my money over 10 years?

As I write, BWP has returned 127 per cent—I'm well on track to tripling my money.

I've used this as an example of the intelligent way to invest in property. It's really quite simple. When I purchased BWP it was earning me an 8 per cent rental return—with no costs—versus an average property investor who earns a 3 per cent return *less* costs.

When it comes to any investment, it's all about the cash in your pocket. Everything else is speculation.

A word of warning

Although BWP Trust was a great deal when I bought it, at the time of writing this book, I no longer advise my subscribers to buy it, because it's gone up so much. I just used it to point out that buying an investment property ain't the only way to make money in property.

Property vs shares

Listen, I don't do Holden vs Ford and I sure as hell don't do property vs shares.

What I do is take an unemotional view of historic returns, together with what actually puts cash in my pocket, and invest accordingly.

Know this: you will hear many weird and wonderful things about investing over your life, mostly from people who want to sell you something and hence have a vested interest in underplaying the risks of borrowing (whether it's for property, shares or emu eggs).

I'm giving you the same advice I give my parents, my sister, my friends and myself.

How to be a hero— investing for your kids (or grandkids)

You may not have kids. You may not even like kids. But you know someone who has kids, right?

Well, you have the ability to change the course of a young person's entire life.

Huh?

According to ASIC, the majority of Australians 'don't have the basic numeracy skills required to meet the demands of everyday life and work'.

That's not you.

You're smart enough to be sitting here with me, reading a finance book, making massive strides to getting your own money sorted.

And I'm guessing that means you probably have a lot of influence over your family and friends when it comes to their money matters (whether you realise it or not). So I'm now going to arm you with every bit of information you need to help change a young person's life.

I count myself extremely privileged to have helped a lot of young people get a handle on money, and I can tell you it's been the most humbling experience of my life.

And now it's your turn.

What follows is a plan to making a difference in a young person's life.

The number one secret to raising financially fit kids is...

...to be a good money manager yourself.

You'll do that by following the Barefoot Steps. Even better, you won't be stressed about money, so you'll have more time to be present with your kids.

As kids get older they may not listen to you—but they never fail to imitate you, so:

- *be a good provider*: show them the joy of hard work, and the respect you gain by doing a good job

- *be thrifty*: show them that lights need to be switched off, and that money is to be saved for a rainy day

- *be an investor*: this is the fun part—unlike most kids, who stare blankly at a compound interest chart in high-school maths—you can show them first hand.

Let's get stuck into it.

The Grow Bucket: compound interest for kids

This investment will form part of your Grow Bucket.

And grow it will: a once-off investment of, say, $2000, plus $50 a week, could be worth more than $140 000 in 21 years' time.

That'll come in handy because for some time private school fees have been growing at twice the rate of inflation. Australian parents spend, on average, $50 000 on their kids' education, according to a report by the National Centre for Social and Economic Modelling.

And many can't afford it.

The *Australian Financial Review* reported that a quarter of parents borrow for their kids' private school education, and one in seven run up a credit card debt to pay for school fees.

So it's not surprising that each year I get hundreds of emails and letters from well-meaning people who want to put some money aside for the kids in their lives.

The problem is, too many of these people screw it up, and then they write to me.

So let me show you how to do it right.

(And if you decide to send your kids to the local state school, you'll be able to give them a bloody big cheque that they'll be able to use as a deposit on a home, or that will give them the freedom to follow their passion and start their own business.)

Straight up, under no circumstances should you invest for your kids' future in a bank account. This especially applies to the accounts designed for kids (which often come with a cute plastic piggybank). They're generally awful, with terms and conditions that give your kids their first lesson on banks being bastards.

Avoid them like broccoli.

Instead, we're going to invest in good-quality Aussie shares.

But it's here that things get a little difficult.

See, the government wants to deter you from using your kids as a tax dodge, so they smack minors who declare 'unearned income'.

The first $416 of their unearned income is tax-free, but after that the penalty tax kicks in and can go as high as 66 per cent (no, that's not a typo).

Thankfully, there are two (perfectly legal) ways to get around paying penalty tax on kids' investments: you can invest in your own name (perfect for lower income earners) or via an investment bond (perfect for higher income earners).

Let's talk about each of these.

Lower income earners

If you or your partner is earning below $37 001 per annum, you should buy shares in a low-cost listed investment company (LIC) like AFIC (ASX: AFI) or Argo (ASX: ARG) on behalf of the kid.

Put it in the lower earning spouse's name.

We've covered share investing in Step 5 already, but let me give you the 30-second recap here:

A LIC is basically a share fund that trades on the sharemarket. The oldest LICs, like AFIC and Argo, have been around for decades (and in the case of AFIC since the 1920s) and have been wonderful investments for long-term investors who don't want the hassle of picking individual shares or paying high management fees.

Bottom line? I have a large amount of my own money in LICs. So do my parents, and my mates and my children (under my name—see below).

You buy the shares in a LIC by opening a share trading account. And if you don't have an account, in most cases your bank will have one. Buying is as simple as doing internet banking. Just make sure you set up your share trading account with the following designation:

Adult

Alan John Wilson

Minor

Penny Wilson A/C

This means you're the legal owner of the shares—and therefore you'll need to declare any income from the shares in your tax return. Still, it's simple and clear (from a records perspective) that you're administering the account on behalf of your child.

For a stay-at-home mum or dad this is a cracker of a strategy because you can earn $18 200 in total income each year before you have to pay any tax on earnings.

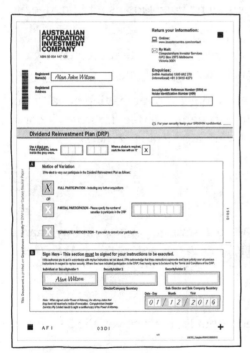

You'd have to have more than $300 000 invested before you even had to think about paying tax. Better yet, you'll even get money back from the unused company tax credits (known as franking credits).

In a few weeks' time you'll get a dividend reinvestment plan (DRP) letter in the mail (like this).

Tick 'full participation'.

This will allow you to automatically reinvest any dividends into buying more shares. When you do this, you won't need to pay brokerage (the fee for buying or selling shares), and often you'll get a slight discount on the current share price.

Higher income earners

What about if each of you is earning over $37000 per annum?

Then the name is Bond…*Investment Bond.*

Bad jokes aside, I'm a huge fan of investment bonds.

They allow you to invest in managed share funds, and they're awesome for kids.

Let me give you three reasons why I had a picture of an investment bond next to my poster of Michael Jordan in my bedroom growing up:

There is no additional capital gains tax (CGT) after 10 years when you sell.

You can open an investment bond, start up a regular savings plan into a managed share fund, compound your returns and then pull your money out capital gains tax free after 10 years.

You can kiss your accountant goodbye (you don't have to declare the income).

The investment bond pays tax within the bond (at the corporate tax rate of 30 per cent—which is why it makes sense for higher income earners), so there's no need to declare this on your yearly tax return. And there's no tax at the end of the 10-year period. Dead simple.

You can compound your yearly contributions.

A major benefit of investment bonds is you can increase your yearly contributions by 25 per cent each year and still pull your money out free of CGT after 10 years.

Which investment bond?

There are a number of investment bond providers—like Lifeplan's NextGen Investments, Austock Life's Imputation Bonds and AMP's Growth Bonds. To choose one, the same rules you used for choosing a super fund apply: you want to invest in shares (not all of them do) and the lower the fees you can pay the better.

The only company I will *not* let you go anywhere near is the Australian Scholarships Group, or ASG, as it's known. ASG is the largest provider of educational scholarship plans in Australia—but biggest in this case does not mean best.

ASG is like the Tooth Fairy (which is hands down the creepiest character that's ever been created to deceive kids). Like the Tooth Fairy, ASG promises to magically appear and leave behind shiny coins. Also, like with the Tooth Fairy, in order to get any money from ASG you have to pay through the teeth.

Look, ASG's scholarships are just awful: their fees and charges are incredibly high.

The bottom line? Stay away from ASG.

One more thing: all bonds have a number of rules, so check the fine print before you invest.

How not to raise a spoilt brat

I'm passionate about financial education.

I even bought a farm for my kids. Each one will get a paddock, a ram and a ewe—financial education and sex education rolled into one.

The trouble parents get into is not understanding that pocket money is really a tool for financial education.

So if you don't want your kids to grow up entitled, don't give them an allowance. Make them pitch in on ordinary things around the house (washing up, taking out the bins), but pay them for working hard (like in the real world).

Now I've already introduced you to the Serviette Strategy with its 'three bucket' approach. For your kids, the three buckets turn into three jam jars.

Grab three jars (without the jam!) and label them 'Spend', 'Save' and 'Give'.

Kids learn by seeing and touching (which is why student banking sucks), so you want to make it as visual as possible. Keep the jars in your kid's room so they can see the money piling up.

Divide the coins evenly:

- *Spend:* kids need to learn how to become savvy shoppers, and the best way to teach them is through experience.

- *Save:* teaching them that they need to save for stuff is the cornerstone of an effective financial education, and pays lifelong dividends.

- *Give:* this is a life lesson in contentment—after all, the happiest people on the planet are those who give. It also teaches children that by living in Australia they're already among the richest people on the planet, and it puts money in its proper perspective.

Older kids can go to kiva.org and help a struggling entrepreneur in the developing world. They can loan $25 online, then follow the entrepreneur's story on the Kiva website. Twenty-five bucks is chicken feed to change the lives of two people: the entrepreneur's and your child's.

Oh, and for teenagers flipping burgers, they'll have outgrown the piggy banks, so they can put their earnings into three separate bank accounts (Spend, Save, Give) instead.

Paris Hilton, Donald Trump and your kids

If you apply the knowledge I've given you, you'll be the VIP at your kid's 21st.

However, if you don't also teach them how to handle money, you'll end up with your very own Paris Hilton ... or Donald Trump—his father was a multimillionaire, you know (*don't even get me started on this*).

Think about it.

What would you have done if your old man handed you a cheque for, say, $140 000 on your 21st birthday?

You'd have developed a sensible, diversified portfolio ... of weed, whisky and women. *Woo-hooo!*

(I didn't get a cheque, or even a dollar coin. In fact, the closest thing to a precious metal I got was an engraved 21st birthday beer stein that was topped up throughout the night, leaving me a heaving mess the next morning.)

No, the aim is to build up their net worth *and* their self-worth.

As you've probably worked out, this book is very personal, so I'm going to explain it to you in the best way I can—by showing you a letter I wrote to my kids.

Feel free to share it with your kids.

A letter to my children

You've all got something that everyone wants a lot more of.

Time.

You see, most people run out of time.

I see it every day in my job: I try to convince young people about just how powerful their lives could be (they don't believe me). I spend the rest of my day trying to help older people who are desperately trying to make up for lost time. They're racing against the clock.

Yet here's the thing: if you have time, you don't have to race. You don't need to nervously check stock prices every day. You don't have financial pressure. You don't need the stock market to do something. You don't get suckered into get-rich-quick schemes. You don't freak out when the market crashes.

You can make time work for you.

And, as your dad, it's my job to show you how to do it.

So, I'm going to give you a bunch of money, a fancy car and a Lear jet.

I'm joking! (Look how well that turned out for Justin Bieber.) My old man didn't give me a silver spoon, and you won't get one from me either. Instead, I'm going to give you a couple of life lessons.

The joy of hard work

Every week for over a decade, I've written a newspaper column.

They pay me the same money whether I bash something out in an hour or a day.

So I could take the easy option. But I don't. Case in point, for one of my columns I spent two days researching, interviewing and writing about how money can keep women trapped in violent relationships. I put my heart and soul into those 987 words.

And it paid off. That article was shared by thousands of people. But, more importantly, I received some incredibly personal, heartwarming—even tragic—emails from women who needed to hear that message of hope: that they weren't alone. That something could be done for them and their kids.

My point is, there's a special joy in hard work. In doing a good job and delivering on your promises.

The miracle of compound interest

Now, let's talk about the simplest and safest way to create your fortune: compound interest.

As you'll learn, there are many, many things your old man can't do (Mum will fill you in later).

But the one thing I have in my favour is I know how compound interest works.

In fact, I don't just know it—I've lived it.

And you can too.

With enough time, you can't help but build enormous wealth. Your greatest investment weapon isn't a high IQ, a knack for numbers, or fancy letters after your name: it's time. And the sooner you start, the better. Take a look at this chart, which tells the story of you and your mate.

Let's say that at age 15 you start working on the family farm.

You work incredibly hard, scrape together $5000 a year and invest it in a basic share fund. You reinvest your dividends for the next 10 years. Along the way you earn a nominal 10 per cent (for the past 30 years shares have actually returned 10.8 per cent a year ... but not in a straight line).

And then you stop.

Your mate doesn't start as early as you. He waits until he gets a real job — at age 25 — before he starts investing. Like you, he puts in $5000 a year but, unlike you, he doesn't stop. He keeps on investing every year until he's 60 years old.

All up, you put in $50000. He puts in $180000.

So you'd think he'd have more than you, right?

Wrong. Even though you've only put in less than one-third the amount he did, you end up with over 50 per cent more! (You get $2709000 — he gets $1645000).

That's the power of compound interest. That's the power of time.

This isn't a new thing. It's not hit and miss. It works every single time, and it's the safest and surest way to become incredibly wealthy. So why don't more people do it?

Well, because it's kinda ... boring.

Most people don't even do the $5000.

(People will always find a reason to 'play it safe' and do nothing. Those people will always be broke.)

Age	You invest:		Your friend invests:	
15	$5,000	$5,500		
16	$5,000	$11,550		
17	$5,000	$18,205		
18	$5,000	$25,526		
19	$5,000	$33,578		
20	$5,000	$42,436		
21	$5,000	$52,179		
22	$5,000	$62,897		
23	$5,000	$74,687		
24	$5,000	$87,656		
25		$96,421	$5,000	$5,500
26		$106,064	$5,000	$11,550
27		$116,670	$5,000	$18,205
28		$128,337	$5,000	$25,526
29		$141,171	$5,000	$33,578
30		$155,288	$5,000	$42,436
31		$170,816	$5,000	$52,179
32		$187,898	$5,000	$62,897
33		$206,688	$5,000	$74,687
34		$227,357	$5,000	$87,656
35		$250,092	$5,000	$101,921
36		$275,102	$5,000	$117,614
37		$302,612	$5,000	$134,875
38		$332,873	$5,000	$153,862
39		$366,160	$5,000	$174,749
40		$402,776	$5,000	$197,724
41		$443,054	$5,000	$222,996
42		$487,359	$5,000	$250,795
43		$536,095	$5,000	$281,375
44		$589,705	$5,000	$315,012
45		$648,675	$5,000	$352,014
46		$713,543	$5,000	$392,715
47		$784,897	$5,000	$437,487
48		$863,387	$5,000	$486,735
49		$949,725	$5,000	$540,909
50		$1,044,698	$5,000	$600,500
51		$1,149,167	$5,000	$666,050
52		$1,264,084	$5,000	$738,155
53		$1,390,493	$5,000	$817,470
54		$1,529,542	$5,000	$904,717
55		$1,682,496	$5,000	$1,000,689
56		$1,850,746	$5,000	$1,106,258
57		$2,035,820	$5,000	$1,222,383
58		$2,239,402	$5,000	$1,350,122
59		$2,463,343	$5,000	$1,490,634
60		$2,709,677	$5,000	$1,645,197

Some who invest will often check their returns after three years, feel they're getting nowhere and decide to 'diversify' into a Honda Jazz, a trip to Bali and an iPhone 98.

(The reality is that most people learn about compound interest in reverse—by buying stuff they don't need, with money they don't have, to impress people they don't care about. Yet debt robs them of their financial independence. Debt makes things more expensive. Ultimately, debt is slavery.)

Hardly anyone makes it to the seventh year, which is when the compounding snowball really starts.

Yet if you can stick with it, that's when your life changes. The money starts pouring in, in gushes.

That's when you'll crack the time code. And that's when you can truly 'tread your own path', as I'm always banging on about.

Love, Dad

The widow who put her kids through private school

Lea Johnson, VIC

Barefoot is constant reiteration that it is okay to question your bank and other providers around getting the best deal.

I was widowed at the ripe old age of 37. I had three children under eight.

My husband died, my accounts were frozen and I had to borrow money from my parents for groceries and house payments. I then moved back to Swan Hill, where my family lives, and started from scratch.

I have always enjoyed reading about financial strategy and the little things (like compound interest) that can make such a difference. So I borrowed *The Barefoot Investor* from the library and I started working on Mojo and making sure I had separate buckets of money for committed expenditure and all the other things I may need or want down the track.

Now I have managed to put two children through private school. My son has just completed VCE and loves Barefoot as much as I do—he's just cross that I didn't make him start investing at the age of nine!

Barefoot is constant reiteration that it is okay to question your bank and other providers around getting the best deal. I now own my house, I have investments, and my children understand how money works and have great respect for their own earnings. We talk about investing, tax deductions, profit and loss, and what it means to be financially literate.

There have been nights when I've woken up in a cold sweat worrying about some of my decisions, but it's always fleeting and has become less of an issue as I now see everything building very nicely.

It's been fabulous.

STEP 6

BOOST YOUR MOJO TO THREE MONTHS

On your first Barefoot Date Night, you opened a Mojo account with $2000.

And now that you've automated your long-term investing, we're back to finish off the job of providing your security in the short term: you're going to point your Fire Extinguisher at your Mojo Bucket and boost it to three months of living expenses.

Your Fire Extinguisher has been used to domino your debts, to save for a house deposit, and now it's going to give you the ultimate trophy: never, ever, having to worry about money again.

If your legacy is looking after your family—being a good provider—this is the step that makes it happen.

With three months of Mojo you're telling the world—telling your family—that you're putting them ahead of your ego. You're buying them safety and security. Very few people ever consciously make that decision.

This move takes character...which is what true wealth is all about.

The power of Mojo—never worry about money again

You and I, we're not very good at figuring out what will make us happy in the long run. If we were, all the stuff we once pined for—that we've now got—would have done the trick, right?

Thankfully, science has an answer for us. Repeated studies have shown that, beyond a basic level of income (around $70000 a year), there's no discernible link between a high income, or a large bank balance, and happiness.

Yet there is a 'hack' to happiness.

There's one thing that researchers from Harvard to Princeton have *repeatedly* found does have a measurable impact on your happiness: savings.

That's because savings equals freedom. When you've got money in the bank, you're free to live life on your own terms. You have the power. You call the shots.

Is your boss a creep?

You can afford to get the hell out of there and wait till you find something better.

Is your brother sick?

You can be the one person he can count on, who can afford to drop everything, fly interstate and look after him.

Has your car broken down?

You can get it fixed without a second thought.

With savings, you don't owe anybody anything. You're free to do whatever the hell you want.

That's the power of savings. It's not just a number; it's a way of living.

Most people have it back-to-front. They think that saving money is a slog. It's not. Living week to week, worry to worry, fight to fight, for your entire bloody life—*that's* a slog.

Back in Step 1, I got you to set up your bank accounts, including starting your Mojo account with $2000.

Now we're *really* going to slam it home.

You've bought your home (in Step 4), and you've secured your long-term 'I've got this' by putting your investing on autopilot (in Step 5). Now it's time to round back, like a good sheepdog, and deal with the here and now.

BAREFOOT DATE NIGHT MENU

Save up 3 months of Mojo

You're probably going to have your work cut out for you tonight.

Why?

Well, experience has taught me that in most marriages there's one person who values safety and security above all else (generally the woman) and another who wants to buy a jetski (generally the bloke).

Look, there are plenty of things you can spend your money on but, as we've discussed, almost everything you buy will only give you a momentary buzz.

Except if you decide to put money into Mojo, that is. The feeling of security that comes with having more than enough money never leaves you. It never wears off. It becomes part of who you are, and colours your entire view of what's possible. It's what gives you your Mojo.

ENTREE:

You're going to boost your Mojo Bucket to three months of living expenses in case of an emergency (and an emergency isn't a trip to Bali because Jetstar is having a sale).

Okay, but how much is that?

Simple. It's whatever you're putting into your Blow Bucket each month—times three.

Write that figure down right now. That's your next goal amount. Now that you've made your biggest purchase and bought a home, you're going to point your Fire Extinguisher (20 per cent of your take home pay) at filling up your Mojo Bucket.

I want you to set up a recurring direct transfer from your Fire Extinguisher account to your Mojo account each payday, until you hit your 'three months of living expenses' figure. You can do that on your phone with most banks. So do it right now.

MAIN COURSE:

As discussed, your main job tonight is to convince your partner just how important it is to have this money in Mojo—even if you never, ever use it. The payoff is that you'll *never, ever* have to worry about money again. You'll be free.

DESSERT:

Let's just say I'll leave it up to you to work out how you can (ahem) convince your partner to see your side of things ...

The Mojo Mumma

Leanne Russell, VIC

I would never go back to having no Mojo.

I just want to be better than my family. Harsh but true.

I never thought having any financial control was possible. I grew up in western Sydney in a debt-laden environment and I just thought that's what life was, because everyone I knew was living it.

When I was 23, I moved to Melbourne without knowing a single person. My family were turning to drugs and alcohol and I had a violent partner.

I had a $5000 maxed-out credit card and a car loan, which I kept borrowing against. The $22000 car loan grew to over $35000.

Then I bought Scott's book, though my life-change did not happen overnight. The one piece of advice that stuck in my head was that you've got to live within your means.

I knew the first step was to get rid of my debts. I tackled the personal loan first, then the credit card.

When I made the last payment, I could not have been prouder of myself. A small achievement, but for a girl from the rough part of Sydney—unfathomable.

Because of my past, I have a deep and burning desire to stabilise my own life. So after I paid off my debts, I kept up the momentum and started a Mojo account.

Every spare bit of change, I'd save. Now I've got more than three months' living expenses, over $30000, in Mojo.

Having savings was not a comfort I'd ever had before I found Barefoot and I would never go back to having no Mojo. To have money in the bank is just hugely comforting. Particularly now that I'm a mother.

I think of my upbringing, when everything was too hard or too expensive, and I want a different future for my son. I want him to understand that over time he can build wealth for himself. And I want his efforts with money to compound from a young age. An opportunity I never had.

I am now working hard to save for a home. I've also started salary-sacrificing into super. These are things I never would have even thought about in my old life.

I guess I'm just a normal person on a normal salary who can achieve good things. I hope so.

I've had to change my thinking from 'maybe I could' to 'this is what I'll do, and by when'. Thinking this way has been the number one Barefoot slap-to-the-head for me. It's all about taking action. Simple ideas that deliver, long term.

You know what, Scott? This is my chance to extend just a heartfelt freaking thank-you!

Recap of Part 2: Grow

You and I have come a long way since we first sat down together.

You're now far ahead of the average person—even those with an expensive financial planner—because you're getting fiercely independent advice, and you're taking total control of your own money.

And while some people get bogged down with cutting out coffees and sticking to budgets, you've instead focused your Barefoot Date Nights on scoring big wins—on the big things that really make a difference.

By the end of Barefoot Step 6 you've:

- made a commitment to boosting your current salary by *at least* $5000 in the next 12 months

- got a paint-by-numbers approach to saving for a deposit and avoiding lenders' mortgage insurance

- called your super fund and put your retirement savings on autopilot at 15 per cent, boosted your end payout by potentially hundreds of thousands of dollars and received a tax deduction in the process

- completely changed your family tree by teaching your kids the power of money, hard work and giving—better yet, securing their financial futures with the investing plan you now have.

Most importantly of all, you're on track to achieve real financial freedom.

With three months of Mojo you'll never ever have to worry about money again. You're in charge. You call the shots. You're free.

Now it's time to reap the rewards and enjoy a feast.

You're growing, and winning.

It's time to harvest!

Part 3
HARVEST

Ask any farmer what their favourite time of the year is, and they'll tell you 'harvest!'

The sun is shining, the birds are chirping...and they're about to get paid!

By the time you've finished your harvest, you'll have crossed off the two biggest goals every Aussie has...but very few achieve.

You're going to get the banker off your back, once and for all.

But, more importantly, you're going to retire in absolute comfort.

And I'm not talking about some young sapling with 35 seasons of compound interest left in him. I'm talking about a 65-year-old who's terrified they've left it too late.

You see, I'm going to show you what I call the Donald Bradman Retirement Strategy. It'll strip away the fear you have about your retirement and reveal how you can retire in comfort regardless of how much money you have in super right now. I guarantee you've never read anything like it.

In Harvest I'm also going to:

- show you how to save $77 641 on your mortgage and wipe out almost seven years of payments

- reveal the dirty secret that the mortgage industry doesn't want you to know

- step out your 'retirement number' and show you how to nail it

- give you the phone numbers of independent financial experts who can help you...not sell you.

Plus you're going to go on a very special Barefoot Date Night.

But now it's time for some apple pie...it's time to harvest!

STEP 7

GET THE BANKER
OFF YOUR BACK

When you get to this step, I want you to go all-out on your next Barefoot Date Night.

Go somewhere really hoity-toity and—what the hell—arrive in one of those stretch limos that only old farts (with lots of money) and young kids (going to their end-of-year formal) bother hiring.

In this step you're going to save tens of thousands with just a few phone calls.

There are only two ways to pay your mortgage off more quickly:

1. Lower your interest rate.

2. Make extra repayments.

We're going to do both.

But first, let me tell you about a phenomenon I call 'postcode povvos'.

The curious case of the postcode povvos

The word 'mortgage', as I've already said, means 'an agreement till death'.

And make no mistake, the entire universe is conspiring against you ever being mortgage-free.

It happens when you watch shows like *The Block*.

It happens when you type 'How much can I borrow?' into a bank's website calculator.

It happens when your friends buy a house in a nicer suburb than yours, and you get a jitter of jealousy.

A side-effect of living through the biggest debt boom in history is that some people view a house like a chess piece: you hold onto it long enough for the equity to rise—and then you trade up to a newer, flashier suburb with newer, flashier neighbours.

I've got a name for people who do this: I call them 'postcode povvos'—people who hock themselves to the hilt so they can live in a fancy suburb, but end up living lives of quiet desperation in the process.

Postcode povvos

Let me introduce you to one such couple...they're friends of ours, although I've changed their details. Obviously.

This couple has been married for about nine years. Two squids. They work in the same skyscraper in the city where they met. They earn decent—but not great—dough.

When they first got married all they could afford to buy was a poky little joint in the meat-and-potatoes suburb of Reservoir, in Melbourne's north.

The day they bought it they didn't celebrate. It was more like the underwhelm you felt as a teenager when you opened the Christmas present from that aunty and uncle you only see once a year: 'You got me a ... Garfield colouring book ... gee ... thanks'.

No, Reservoir was just a layover on the road to someplace better ... and that better place was pricey Port Melbourne.

Over the next eight years they'd talk longingly and lovingly about Port Melbourne, where their other, richer friends lived. It was like everything that went wrong in their lives was caused by being 'stuck' in Reservoir.

(We, on the other hand, lived in the country, in one of the poorer parts of greater Melbourne—far, far away from the pristine waters of Port Melbourne ... 'though we do have dams', I'd jokingly tell them.)

Everything would be *perfect* when they moved to Port Melbourne. Life would be like a choreographed Instagram feed:

He'd have a ripped sixpack because every morning he'd get up and kayak along the bay, while she'd get into her Lorna Jane active wear and meditate as she looked out to the ocean. They'd spend their weekends frollicking with their kids on the beach, and at dusk they'd have a BBQ, drink chardonnay and toast the good life.

Winner, winner, chicken dinner, right?

Well, lo and behold, the little place in Reservoir shot up in price like a rocket. They sold for a record price, but again they didn't celebrate. They still didn't get enough to buy the place they really wanted (which of course had gone way up too).

However, they were determined to live their Instagram fantasy, so they traded up and bought a poky little joint in Port Melbourne two streets back from the water—and in the process added more than $1 million to their mortgage.

What do you think happened next?

Like for most people who borrow too much for their dream home, the Windex had worn off and she was left stressed to the max, while he decided to 'take control' of their money and didn't tell her much—which made her paranoid.

'What are you going to do about it?' I asked her one day when she was having a coffee.

'I guess I'm just used to living this way,' she sighed, slouching her shoulders, looking down at her latte.

'So,' I said, 'you're sitting here, as one of the richest people on the planet, and you're telling me you're okay spending the next 50 years worried about money?'

'It's not so bad. Everyone is in the same position … right?' she said.

Actually, no …

The millionaire next door

One of the best books on the postcode povvo phenomenon is *The Millionaire Next Door*.

The authors, Thomas J Stanley and William D Danko, set out to study the buying habits of the very wealthy. They began by interviewing people they perceived as rich: those in wealthy suburbs with big homes, expensive cars and all the other trappings of success.

Yet their findings were puzzling. The people they interviewed had high incomes, but they were asset poor. Worse, they were drowning in debt. In other words, they were 'all show and no dough'.

So the authors changed tack and began searching for people who were genuinely wealthy. And what they found ran contrary to what society says a successful millionaire looks like.

Real millionaires, they found, create their fortunes by following the time-tested rules of wealth (which, incidentally, mirror the Barefoot Steps). They are long-term investors—a whopping 95 per cent own shares. They avoid credit cards. They save. They don't have boats, lap pools or Porsches. And they drive second-hand family cars, the equivalent of a Falcon or Commodore.

And now the clincher: the wealthy people they interviewed were living in modest homes, in modest middle-class suburbs—hence the title of the book, *The Millionaire Next Door*.

Don't do it for the kids

So what's become of our postcode povvo pals?

Well, 'one point four' didn't buy them a really nice home in Port Melbourne...so they're already talking and dreaming about trading up to something a bit... *bigger*.

I've seen how this plays out. It never ends.

There's always someone with a bigger house than yours (unless you're the Queen, and she's got her own problems—look at her family!).

So let's turn it on its head:

They're paying tens of thousands of dollars in interest to the bank.

They could instead spend that money on an unforgettable overseas family holiday each year: take the kids out of school, hire a campervan and drive across America for six weeks.

Or, if they didn't have their mortgage migraine, they could afford to take their foot off the accelerator—slow the hell down—and free up some time to coach their kids' footy team.

And that's the rub: if you ask this couple why they've got themselves into home loan hell, they'll say it's for their kids.

But their kids don't give two hoots about their fancy home in their fancy suburb.

All they want is to spend time with their parents.

All they want is their parents to stop fighting about money all the time.

I grew up in the Mallee town of Ouyen—smack bang in the middle of nowhere—in a little home my parents built themselves (out of what in retrospect looked suspiciously like asbestos sheeting), and I had the time of my life, because my parents were always around.

Don't get me wrong: I'm not against trading up, but I am here to tell you that signing up to a mega-mortgage for the next three decades just so I can live in a 'rich' suburb is not a trade-off I'm willing to make.

There's not a home in the world that will make you as happy as being in control of your time. That's true freedom. And the sooner you can wipe your mortgage, the sooner you can live life on your terms.

How to save $77 641 and wipe almost seven years off your mortgage

If your home loan is with a big bank, there's a good chance you're getting screwed. Generally speaking, the banks don't do the best deals on home loans because…they don't need to. So let's talk about what you really need from your home loan.

Rule 1: Don't get the bells and whistles

A home loan is a pretty simple proposition: you borrow money from the bank to buy a home, and then pay it back with interest over 25 to 30 years.

Most of the bells and whistles the banks market as 'special features' are rubbish—their main purpose is to bamboozle you into paying more for things you rarely use. So stay away from repayment holidays, fixing a portion of your loan and anything else dreamed up by a marketing dude with a ponytail. This is where the banks make their margins.

Rule 2: Don't fix your rate

Repeat after me: 'I promise to stick with the lowest variable rate I can find, regardless of what my brother-in-law Eric recommends at Christmas lunch'.

> **Here's what Eric will say:** Man, I got a great deal on a fixed rate—and it's locked in for five years.
>
> **Here's your reply:** Yes, Eric, the banks are offering fantastic fixed-rate deals, many lower than the standard variable—and there's a reason. It's not because they want to help you pay off your loan quicker. Rather, since the government banned exit fees, the banks have had to find another way to stop their customers switching to a better deal. Fixed-rate loans give them that power. And, Eric, if interest rates drop lower than your fixed rates and you want to switch banks, your bank will slug you with a 'break fee', representing the difference between the two rates, multiplied by the length of time left on your fixed contract—which can add up to thousands of dollars.

So much for Eric.

The only reason you'd fix your rate is if you're really struggling (like Eric) and you want the security of fixed repayments, but for everyone else it's too much of a gamble.

Rule 3: Get the cheapest rate possible

Truth is, just as with many relationships, it's easier to bitch to your current bank than it is to go through the hassle of switching to another one.

Which brings me to your first phone call for this monthly Barefoot Date Night...

The $22 064 phone call

Here's the deal: it costs your bank about $1000 in marketing costs to replace you (and about six times that amount if you come via a mortgage broker they pay kickbacks to).

That's your negotiating power right there.

Here's how to use it.

First, I want you to google 'UBank Home Loan Rate'.

Second, call your bank, ask for the 'customer retention department' and use this script:

> **You:** Hello, my account number is _____. I've been with you for ____ years, but I've applied to refinance with UBank. Their rate is ____ per cent, which is a full ____ per cent cheaper than you're charging me. Given our longstanding relationship, I'd like you to match the offer—or send me the forms I need to switch to UBank.
>
> **Bank rep:** One moment, please.

(You're bluffing, of course. However, the bank's sales team have strict targets, backed by incentives, that they have to meet—one of which is giving profitable customers discounts to stop them leaving.)

> **Bank rep:** We can't match the rate you have quoted. However, we understand you are a valuable customer, so we would like to offer you a 0.15 per cent discount.
>
> **You:** That's not good enough. I've already got conditional approval...so in order to stay I need at least a 0.5 per cent discount. Could you please speak to your supervisor? I'm happy to wait.
>
> **Bank rep (a full six minutes later):** On reviewing your case, we can offer you that 0.5 per cent discount on your current rate.
>
> **You:** Brilliant! Please send me an email confirming the new rate and confirming that it will be applied as of start of business tomorrow.

This phone call works

This phone call can save you $22064 in interest (based on a $400000 mortgage over 18 years at 4 per cent). Over the years I've had plenty of readers do this exact negotiation on the phone (even on their way home from work) and in most cases they've reported back that they've saved themselves a huge amount of money.

But what if your bank says no?

Easy. Ring them again.

What if they say no again?

Don't bitch, switch. (As long as you have more than 20 per cent equity in your home. If you don't, you'll get hit with another round of LMI, which will eat up any savings you can negotiate.)

Now, here's how to hunt for the best mortgage.

Straight up, if you're going for your first home, check out the online players like UBank and ING, which generally have the cheapest rates (although you'll need to have a 20 per cent deposit and a solid savings history).

But what if you've got a more complicated set-up—like being self-employed, or having multiple loans? In that case you need a mortgage broker—but not just any mortgage broker...

Revealed: the mortgage industry's dirty little secret

When you get a loan through a mortgage broker, they don't charge you anything.

But make no mistake, they still get paid—and in two ways: the bank they recommend pays them an upfront commission (around $3000 on an average loan), and then they get a 'trailing commission' (read: kickback) for the life of your loan (up to $1000 a year, every year).

The solution is to get a broker who'll charge you an upfront fee (which is a fair cop for their expertise) but will *refund* the trailing commission off your mortgage.

They're called 'cash-back mortgage brokers'. I used them when I bought my farm, and, when the cash-back was kicked-back to my loan each month, I got the same buzz I assume a pokie-punter gets when they score 'five free spins' on the pokies.

(Most mortgage brokers hate me for highlighting their kickback structure—some have threatened me with physical violence.)

Why on earth would some mortgage brokers offer such a good deal? Well, very few do, but there's a select few (see page 230 for a list of independent financial professionals you can hook up with...just like on Tinder) who see it as an ethical differentiation from their kickback-collecting counterparts.

Point the Fire Extinguisher at your home loan

So we've got you the cheapest variable rate on the market. Now it's time for part two: making extra repayments.

Where are you going to find the money to make the extra repayments?

Well, let's have a quick recap of the Barefoot Steps.

In Step 2, you arranged to have 20 per cent of your take-home pay put into your Fire Extinguisher account, to be used for putting out 'financial fires'.

In Step 3, you pointed that Fire Extinguisher at your debts.

In Step 4, you pointed that Fire Extinguisher at a deposit to save up and buy your home.

In Step 6, you pointed that Fire Extinguisher at your Mojo Bucket and topped it up to three months of living expenses.

We're now at Step 7 and you're going to point that Fire Extinguisher at your mortgage repayments, so you can 'hose them down' once and for all.

If you pay just $1000 extra (on top of your minimum repayment) a month off your home loan, along with getting a cheaper rate, you'll save $77 641 in interest and wipe almost seven years off your mortgage (based on a $400 000 mortgage over 18 years). To work out exactly how much you can save, head over to ASIC's MoneySmart Mortgage Calculator and do the sums with your own mortgage.

The proudest day of my financial life

I used to describe my mortgage as 'like wearing a pair of really nice but really tight shoes'. Sure, they looked good, but they made every step painful, and I couldn't wait to get home, kick off my shoes and tread my own path.

Let me tell you about the day I got the banker off my back.

Now, I could have made the final transfer via internet banking, but I didn't.

Bugger that.

I had visions of entering into my local branch—strutting in like a peacock—and my bank manager would greet me at the door with a little sponge cake she'd bought from Woolies on her way to work that morning, to mark this momentous day. And behind her the entire branch would gather in a circle and start clapping, and then balloons would fall from the ceiling and they'd yell, 'Speech! Speech', and I'd act all surprised and gracious...while I *was secretly loving every minute of it.*

That's not what happened. Here's how it actually went down:

> **Barefoot:** I'd like to make the final payment on my mortgage and close my account, please.
>
> **Teller:** Okay. (Silence, other than the tappety-tap of her keyboard.)
>
> **Barefoot:** It's a nice feeling… to pay off my mortgage.
>
> **Teller:** Uh-huh. One moment.

The teller went over and spoke to the bank manager, and a minute later they both came back to the little glass window where I was standing.

> **Bank manager:** Hello, Mr Pape. I've got to warn you that it's actually not a prudent idea to close off your home loan.
>
> **Barefoot:** Why?
>
> **Bank manager:** Well, think about it. You now have an opportunity to build your wealth by buying an investment property—or some shares—using the equity of your home, and we already have this facility in place.
>
> **Barefoot:** Just discharge my mortgage and give me back my title…
>
> **Bank manager:** That's the thing. It actually costs you a lot to discharge your mortgage, but it costs you nothing to keep a line-of-credit facility just in case…
>
> **Barefoot:** I'm going to frame it, and put it on my wall.
>
> **Bank manager:** You're in the minority… most customers…
>
> **Barefoot:** This is one of the proudest days of my life. I'll happily pay the fee. This is not a negotiation.

That night, Liz and I celebrated, and I swear the grass under my bare feet felt different.

And once you get the banker off your back, it'll be the same for you too.

BAREFOOT DATE NIGHT MENU

Get the banker off your back

This is going to be a big payday for you, so I want you to go somewhere really cool for your Barefoot Date Night (preferably a joint where the staff don't wear name tags). Because by the end of the night you're going to be really proud of yourself.

ENTREE:

Make the $22 064 phone call to your bank. Follow the script on page 202 word for word.

What if they say no?

Easy. Just ring them again. Talk to someone else. Go on. You've got time before your main arrives.

What if they say no again?

It's highly unlikely they won't give you at least some sort of discount—the squeaky wheel generally gets the oil (just ask Shane Warne). Research from comparison site finder.com.au reveals that of the people who (like you) spend half an hour visiting their bank about their home loan, *four out of five* are successful in getting a better rate.

However, if you're not getting any love whatsoever, it could be because you haven't yet built up enough ownership (equity) in your property. If that's the case, stick with your current lender until you've paid down more of your mortgage, preferably 20 per cent, so you don't get hit with LMI.

MAIN COURSE:

Look at the picture you drew of your buckets back on page 75. We're now at Step 7 and you're going to use your Fire Extinguisher to hose down your mortgage repayments.

Of course, you're still making the minimum payments from your Blow account; what I'm talking about is the payments on top of the minimum, and it's these that come from your Fire Extinguisher.

Next, whip out for your phone and google 'ASIC MoneySmart Mortgage Calculator' and type in your details (current mortgage, current interest rate and extra repayments from your Fire Extinguisher). It'll calculate how much you'll save in dollars and how many years it'll wipe off your mortgage.

DESSERT:

It's time to get loose: Jägerbombs.

Most people have a home loan. Very few people go through this process of systematically knocking down their mortgage, and that's exactly how your lender likes it. (They're more than happy for your neighbour to spend an extra six years paying off his mortgage.)

Not you, though. You're on your way.

Bottoms up!

The debt-free 40-something millionaires next door

Mark and Donna Gittins, VIC

I'm 41, with a family, and completely debt-free, with assets fast approaching $1 million.

When I was just 13, I wanted to live on a golf course with my own motorised golf cart.

When I was 27, I had a bad credit rating, no savings, no job and no home. Then I met my beautiful wife, Donna, and my life and finances started improving.

When I was 32, my dream became a reality. We built our dream home, paying $175 000 outright for the land … and guess where it was? Backing onto the manicured greens of the tenth hole!

We were keen to ensure the debt was well within our ability to pay, so we managed to keep the mortgage to just under $300 000 for the build. We didn't build a big, expensive home and the fixtures were inexpensive.

With three young kids there was no point spending money on expensive furniture, so we filled our brand-new home with 'hand me downs'. This was difficult, given everyone—including the banks—wanted us to build bigger and borrow more.

But we stuck to our plan. Over time, it becomes weirdly addictive and, eventually, life-changing.

In the early years, our progress was slow but we knew if we stuck to our plan we would get there.

And eventually, we did. We paid off the mortgage in eight years and eight months.

We no longer discuss bills; we just pay them. It's a huge relief to know we can fund any unexpected bill without stress. Our savings and investments are mostly on autopilot and Donna enjoys planning our four family holidays every year. We feel grateful and proud that we can provide for our children and plan holidays without stressing about the cost.

We are young parents unburdened by debt and so we can give our three young children the best education and opportunities in life. We enjoy the picturesque views overlooking the lake and putting green, and I especially love taking my children out in the golf cart every Friday night.

Now I'm 41, with a family, and completely debt-free, with assets fast approaching $1 million. All on the back of some basic Barefoot principles, discipline and sacrifice.

STEP 8

NAIL YOUR RETIREMENT NUMBER

100
NOT OUT!

When you get up to Step 8, for your monthly Barefoot Date Night I want you to go out to a steak restaurant—because we're going to slay some sacred retirement cows, put 'em on the grill and have a feast!

For some of you, what follows will be the most important thing you ever read in your financial life. This section is going to be a revelation…it'll put an end to that little voice in the back of your head that says, 'I am going to have to survive on Aldi dog food in retirement'. You see, if you're reading this section in your 50s, 60s or 70s, it will strip away the fears you have about retirement.

If you're in your 20s, 30s or 40s, you're going to be fine—as long as you follow the Barefoot Steps. If you do, your retirement is going to be a total creampuff. But there's a good chance you have parents, grandparents, family or friends who are close to retirement, so I want you to share this information with them.

I'm going to lay out for you what I call the 'Donald Bradman Retirement Strategy'. It's called this because it's built on the expectation that you'll still be confidently at the crease when you're 100—not out!

The Donald Bradman Retirement Strategy—why you don't need $1 million to retire

The aim of the Donald Bradman Retirement Strategy is simple: to ensure you'll never run out of money.

However, to do that we're going to turn traditional retirement planning on its head. And we're also going to flip the bird at financial planners who say 'you need $1 million to retire'.

I'm going to show you how my Donald Bradman Retirement Strategy took a 65-year-old couple, with $200000 combined in super, and gave them a comfortable retirement... much better than most retirees achieve.

I doubt you've ever read anything quite like this.

Strap your pads on. Grab your bat. It's time to take a swing at the biggest fear people have.

Give us a hand, cobber

When I was a self-conscious teenager, my father imparted cruel and sadistic punishment by driving me around in a 20-year-old, rust-ridden clunker Hilux he'd owned since his 20s. Thankfully, my mother was not impressed with the ute. She put pot-plants in the tray and threatened to turn it into a garden ornament unless he got rid of it. He did.

Fast forward to a few months after my house burned down. I'm with my dad and we're driving through the paddocks... in my very own beaten-up 20-year-old Hilux... surveying the burnt-out fences that would need to be replaced.

'What do you think about my retirement?' he asked.

At that point it dawned on me that I'd been busy helping everyone else but hadn't really spoken to my own parents about their retirement. I felt like the dentist whose kids have crooked teeth. Or the plastic surgeon whose wife has droopy boobs. Thankfully, my parents are on track for a wonderful retirement—and so are you.

Fear and loathing

'You need $1 million in retirement,' say most financial planners.

'$2 million might not even be enough,' wrote a financial planner in the newspaper recently.

Stop!

If you're in your 50s these retirement figures will likely scare the bejeezus out of you. After all, the average Aussie couple retires with $200000 in super.

You do *not* need a million dollars in super to retire

A million dollars is way above what you actually need. At a minimum, you need a paid-off home (see Step 7) plus:

Couples: $250000 in super

Singles: $170000 in super.

Make this your 'retirement number'.

To be clear, this is the number you need to nail before you even think about retiring—and that's in addition to owning your own home outright.

(A note to future readers. If you're reading this in 2027, the amounts you need to save will be affected by inflation, but the same rules apply. It's a very achievable figure.)

Hang on, what if you don't have $250000 before you retire?

You keep working.

Hang on, what if you have more than $250000 saved up in super?

You keep smiling. Barefoot Rule 3445 states: 'When it comes to your retirement, you will *always* be better off having more money in super. Always'.

> **Here's you:** I think old Barefoot needs a pedicure! I mean, really, what sort of retirement will $250000 get us? We don't want to dine out on dog food!
>
> **Here's me:** If you follow my strategy to the letter, you're going to have a very comfortable retirement.
>
> **Here's you (crossing your arms):** Your idea of retirement might be a little different from ours, young man.
>
> **Here's me:** Okay, well let me paint you a picture of what a paid-off home and $250000 (or $170000 for singles) buys you in terms of lifestyle in retirement.

What your retirement will look like

- You enjoy a three-week trip to Noosa each year with your friends, staying in a nice hotel.

- You regularly eat out at nice restaurants, and you choose whatever you want on the menu.

- You enjoy a nice glass of wine (or two) as the sun sets each night.

- You own a near-new Toyota Corolla.

- You regularly buy nice new clothes.

- You continue going to the same hairdresser you always went to while you were working (they're an absolute magician at hiding the grey, and—let's be honest—they've got a bit more work to do these days).

- You keep track of the footy scores on your iPad … and download the occasional dirty movie.

- You enjoy fishing with the latest gear. Your wife goes to Pilates once a week, and you both go to art class and learn how to draw nudes.

- You buy your grandkids nice presents, without spoiling them. More importantly, you buy an annual zoo pass and take them out on day trips. Lots of snaps on the iPhone for the weekly battle of 'my grandkids are cuter than yours' at the golf club.

- You've got enough dough to replace your drab kitchen and bathroom when you retire (you'll be spending a lot more time in the toilet, old boy... drip, drip, drip).

- You've got top-quality private health insurance so you can have your choice of doctor and hospital.

- You've got emergency money socked away so you don't have to worry about day-to-day bills—and you know your long-term income will never run out.

Again, just to be clear, that's what you can look forward to if you retire with a paid-off home and $250000 (or $170000 for singles), if you follow my Donald Bradman Retirement Strategy.

Sound good?

Well, you'll be pleased to know I haven't plucked any of this out of thin air.

What I've just described (minus the dirty movies) is what the stodgy Association of Superannuation Funds of Australia (ASFA) has calculated as being achievable for retirees living a 'comfortable retirement'.

So how much dough does ASFA calculate that this comfortable retirement will cost?

$60264 a year for couples.

$42764 a year for singles.

Now there's a mountain of psychological research that suggests that once you earn over $40000 a year it won't add to your happiness. But, hey, with the improvements in healthcare, you could spend more time in retirement than you did in the workforce—so why not be comfortable, right?

But it gets better.

With Don Bradman on your side, you'll never ever run out of money.

At this point you're thinking, 'Does this plan of yours involve me holding up convenience stores with cricket bats? Because I can't see how my $250 000 will afford me a $60 264 per year lifestyle'.

Let's head to the crease.

Introducing the Donald Bradman Retirement Strategy

This strategy works for everyone, regardless of how much they have in super.

What we're focusing on is getting you to a comfortable retirement, which ASFA says costs:

$60 264 a year for couples or $42 764 for singles.

As I've said, if you can't explain your financial plan in 30 seconds—or sketch it on the back of a serviette—you really don't have a financial plan at all.

Thankfully, there are only three steps to achieving a comfortable retirement.

Rule 1: You must have the banker off your back

This strategy only works if you retire debt free…as in no mortgage (which is why we've already dealt with paying off your mortgage in Step 7).

Even better, the age pension doesn't take into account the value of your family home. (Which means that, theoretically, James Packer could cash in his chips when he's older, buy a $7 billion home and collect the age pension.)

You need to own your own home—debt free—before you retire.

Rule 2: Nail your number

You can't retire until you've nailed your retirement number as a minimum (more money is better): $250 000 in super for couples and $170 000 for singles.

Hang on, what's so special about these numbers?

This is the maximum dollar amount of assets (excluding your family home) that you can have and still get close to the maximum rate of age pension. At the time of writing, the maximum rate of age pension is $35 573.20 per year for couples and $23 597.60 for singles. And it will get you 60 per cent of the way towards your comfortable retirement number on its own.

Think of this as your safety net: it's guaranteed by the government, it's indexed twice a year to keep up with inflation and it will be paid until the day you die.

In other words, if your assets are worth less than $250 000 or so—excluding your family home—that's the gift that pension-age retirees receive from the government by virtue of living in the greatest country on earth.

Hang on.

From experience, I know that last paragraph has probably made you spit out your Tetley's tea, especially if you're what's known as an 'in-betweener'—someone who has slogged away and saved up enough money in super that you don't qualify for the pension, but not enough to be 'rich'.

I have two answers for you:

First, you will *always* be ahead financially if you don't need to qualify for the age pension. That's the way the system's designed—as a safety net only.

Second, as someone who pays my fair share of taxes—something I'll continue to do for decades to come—the idea of 'welfare' rubs me the wrong way. I'm certainly not planning on relying on the pension in my retirement. And anyone under the age of 50 who reads this book and puts in place the Barefoot Steps won't have to either.

However, I'm a financial advisor, not a politician, and my job is to help you and your family and friends live comfortably within the rules. In my opinion, the government will not get rid of the age pension (besides, comparatively, Australia spends less on its pension safety net than many other countries), though they will limit who can get it. As they bloody well should.

Let's take a look at the retirement scoreboard so far.

1. You've paid off your home.

2. You're getting the age pension of $35 573.20 (per couple) a year, indexed for life. And you've got $250 000 in super. (Which will allow you to draw a tax-free income of $12 500 a year; I'll explain exactly how to invest it in the next few pages.)

So, you're now at $48073.20 per year. Even better, this money is guaranteed to keep up with inflation, and it'll last until the day you call stumps.

And you're closing in on your 'comfortable' target of $60264 for a couple.

Let's keep going.

Rule 3: Never, ever retire

It's said that the two most dangerous years of your life are the year you're born and the year you retire.

Well, it looks like you made it through the first one, so let's talk about the second.

The golden rule of retirement is … keep working.

That doesn't mean you have to keep your existing job (especially if you're a tiler with dodgy knees).

You can do something less labour-intensive — just a day or so a week, and it doesn't need to be every week.

Work is good for you: retirees who continue doing some kind of part-time work are found to be the happiest and the least likely to suffer depression.

Why not use the skills you've honed over your career to do some useful work?

I meet so many Uber drivers who are well-to-do retirees who don't need the money — they just like chatting to people and earning their keep at the same time.

And better yet, if you do work, the government will bend over backwards to help you.

Once you reach pension age, you'll not only be able to draw a tax-free pension from your super, but in addition a couple can earn up to $28974 each without paying a cent of income tax (singles can earn $32279 per year).

Yet what if your advisor says, 'You're a winner, you don't have to work another day in your life'.

Barefoot says, 'Work anyway, even if it's a day a week'. The biggest mistake you'll make with your retirement is to give up working.

You'll never, ever, run out of money

Let's take a final look at the retirement scoreboard, after you've applied all three rules:

1. You've paid off your home.

2. You're getting the age pension of $35 573.20 (per couple) a year, indexed for life.

    And you've got $250 000 in super. (After you turn 65, you're legally required to draw down a minimum 5 per cent of your account balance—or in this case $12 500 of tax-free income per year. As you get older, the minimum you're required to drawn down gradually increases.)

3. You and your partner each work just one day a fortnight (and not every fortnight—you'll be in Noosa, remember) to bring in a combined $13 000 a year, completely tax free.

    How?

    You can earn $6500 a year via the Centrelink 'work bonus' without it reducing a cent of your age pension (and thanks to the 2018 Budget it's set to rise to $7800 on 1 July 2019). But, at the time of writing, that's $13 000 a year combined.

Age pension:	$35 573.20
Super pension:	$12 500
Work:	$13 000
Total:	**$61 073.20**

That's *more* than what you need for a comfortable retirement! Ker-ching!

The three-bucket retirement solution

Let's talk about how you should manage your buckets...before you kick the bucket!

You understand how the buckets work while you're working, right? Well when you retire, you're going to operate your buckets from within your superannuation.

Think of it this way: it's like you're a grey nomad who's been invited to Woodstock. When you get there, you pitch your tent. Then you like it so much, you stay there!

Now replace 'Woodstock' with 'superannuation' and you get the idea. And in this magical place there is no taxation, and you're pitching your 'tax-free tent' here—well, up to the $1.6 million cap, anyway. (No joints, guitars or free love—but there's possibly a health care card, and tax-free income for life!)

You've been used to saving up some 'safety money' in your Mojo account, but now you can do this inside super. You're picking up your Mojo and moving it into a similar savings account inside super. From now on, your Mojo Bucket is inside your Grow Bucket.

And you can manage your money inside your super fund exactly the same way you manage your money currently. The only difference is that you'll now...pay no freaking tax (unless you're really rich).

A quick recap:

Your Blow Bucket remains the same; that's still for everyday expenses (which you'll access with your everyday transaction account). And feeding this, in part, will be pension payments from your Grow Bucket.

Your Mojo Bucket, however, now sits inside your Grow Bucket. And what's more, it will go from having three months of living expenses to three *years* of living expenses.

Huh?

Sounds like a lot of money, right?

Yes, it is.

You're no longer working, so you need to be even safer. Here's the thing: knowing that you have three to five years worth of money socked away is going to stop you from having a lot of sleepless nights when the markets get rocky. That Mojo will buy you time to ride out the storm. It will give you a feeling of safety and security—and control.

Now if you're a Collingwood supporter, you're probably quite comfortable with losing, so you may only need three years of living expenses. If you're inclined to freak out and sell at the bottom of the market, shoot for having five years of pension payments.

Where will you get three years of pension payments for Mojo?

Easy peasy.

In the three years leading up to your retirement, you should direct your Fire Extinguisher into maxing out your pre-tax super contributions (your Grow Bucket, that is).

And here's the important part:

These three years of super contributions should be invested into 'cash', not 'shares'.

So, I want you to call your low-cost super fund and tell them that you want anything you contribute, in the three years before you retire, put into a cash account within super. Which we're going to call…drum roll please…your 'Mojo'. (Same 'safety money' it's always been, but now within super.)

There's another very smart reason to devote the last few years of your working life to boosting your Mojo. Could you imagine working your guts out in the three years before you retire, only to have the sharemarket crash the day you slap on the sandals and socks?

Remember, when you're retired you're effectively turning the tap to a dribble (but never completely off—you need to keep working—even if it's just to keep the old grey matter ticking over!), so you need to be conservative.

And the upside of having three years of pension payments in Mojo is that it allows the rest of your money to be put to work and earn a better return.

Your Grow Bucket is also where the remainder of your money should be invested. Specifically, it should be invested in good-quality, dividend-paying shares or share funds within your…again…ultra-low-cost super fund (see Step 1).

These shares will continue to earn dividends. And here's a final trick: I want you to automatically divert all dividends into your Mojo Bucket (which is now inside the Grow Bucket) so that your Mojo's being automatically replenished.

In retirement your biggest risk is that you'll outlive your savings. You need to stay ahead of the rising costs of living, and historically, the only reliable way to do that is by investing long-term in the sharemarket and getting these dividends.

Besides, you can't work forever.

And if you're lucky enough to find yourself under the lights of the MCG on a balmy summer's evening and you're 100 not out, that Mojo will provide an extra level of padding.

Now, go back to page 215 and read about your comfortable retirement again.

Go on…I'll wait.

There's no reason to be afraid.

You've got this.

Everything you want to know about the Donald Bradman Retirement Strategy — in one-and-a-bit pages

What if the government cuts the age pension?

It won't.

Can you really imagine any politician getting re-elected if they cut the sole source of income for the largest voting demographic? Of course not.

Will the government change the low-tax status of super?

It will. It's inevitable. Politicians from both sides have form on stuffing around with super. Every year super will become a little less attractive. But they still have to provide us a carrot to get us to save and not be totally reliant on the age pension.

What if I don't have $250 000 (or $170 000 as a single)? Should I downsize my home?

Sure, why not? Then you could buy something cheaper and put the balance into super. Remember, the value of your house is exempt from the age pension assets test. Your other option is to keep working full time for the next few years until you nail your number. The government encourages older people to continue working by allowing them to draw on their super while they work. This results in you paying less tax — allowing you to sock more money into super.

How much Mojo do I need in retirement?

You should sock away between three and five years of pension payments in cash or fixed interest.

Why should I bother saving at all? The government will just reduce my pension

You've been listening to talkback radio, haven't you? Having more money in retirement is always better. Yes, if you save a lot you'll lose some (or all) of the pension, but that's because you'll be much better off!

How do I know I'll get the full rate of pension?

There are experts you can sit down with—for free—who will help you maximise the amount of pension you receive. In fact, I'll give you their numbers on page 230.

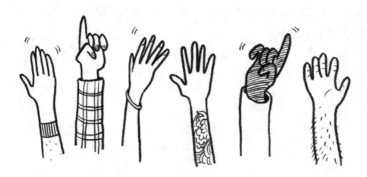

BAREFOOT DATE NIGHT MENU

Nail your number

Tonight you're going to nail your number. There's no need to go to 'pensioner night' at the pub—your retirement is going to be a snap after you create a plan to nail your number.

ENTREE:

Work out how much you currently have in super.

MAIN COURSE:

Next, whip out for your phone and google 'ASIC MoneySmart Retirement Calculator'.

Type in your details—your age, your expected retirement age, your annual income, current super balance, investment choice (balanced) *and*, most importantly, the extra repayments you can now make from your Fire Extinguisher.

It'll calculate how much income you'll likely have in retirement. Play around with the variables and see what adding extra money will do to your end balance.

DESSERT:

Chocolate.

(You'll be eating a lot of that in retirement.)

As you're munching away, read on so you can jump online and find yourself a strapping (often free!) financial advisor to flirt with.

Finding your financial advisor on Tinder

Picture this.

You're on a first date with a bloke called Simon.

As you enter the restaurant, your first impression is that he looks like a nice guy. He's wearing a suit. He's smiling. He looks trustworthy.

Then he opens his mouth...

> **Simon:** So tell me about your goals... and your income... and your assets.
>
> **You:** That's a bit forward. I thought we were just getting to know each other...
>
> **Simon:** We are! But before we can proceed you need to sign this letter of authority. Think of it like a marriage contract—it entitles me to a percentage of your assets for as long as we stay together.
>
> **You:** That sounds like a *very* bad deal for me... what do I get out of it?
>
> **Simon:** We'll meet up once a year and I'll show you my pie chart.
>
> **You:** This is moving too fast for me. All I wanted to do was ask you a few questions about...

Simon (sighing): Look, for a one-night stand I charge $4000. But, honestly, I've moved on from all that. Truth is I'm really not that interested unless you sign the contract and I can get my hands on your assets.

You: Well, can you at least guarantee me higher returns?

Simon: Oh sure…but…not in writing. The truth is that the managed funds I select for you only have a 20 per cent chance of beating a basic index fund…which is understandable, given I'm taking an additional 1 per cent straight off the top—whether your balance goes up, down or sideways.

You: I'm going home now, Simon.

Simon (ogling your assets): Look, wait. You don't understand. I really need this relationship right now. It'd be good for me…

You: Goodbye, Simon.

Ludicrous, right?

Sure, but this is essentially how the financial planning industry operates. Has done for decades.

But if you think that's weird, let's take a look at the way they charge for their services.

Let's say you have $500 000 in assets.

If you're charged a standard 1 per cent financial advisory fee, that'll be $5000 a year.

Now let's say I go to the same advisor, but I have $1 million in assets.

I'm paying the same rate of 1 per cent, which means I'll get the exact same service and the exact same funds as you—but I'll be charged $10 000 a year.

That's like a fat dude walking into a restaurant and the waiter saying, 'Hello sir! Given you're over 130 kilos, we will be charging you *double* for everything on the menu'.

'But,' protests the fat dude, 'I'll be eating the same bowl of pasta as that Kate Moss lookalike is eating over there! Why am I being charged more?'

'Because you're fat, sir,' says the waiter.

Even more ludicrous, right?

Well, let's run the maths.

With $500000 invested in a share fund growing at around the long-term average, how much do you think that 1 per cent annual advisor fee will cost you over the next 20 years?

Let's play *The Price is Right*.

Will you pay $100000 to the advisor?

Higher!

$200000?

Higher!

$300000?

Higher!

Over 20 years of investing $500000 in a share fund, that 1 per cent your advisor charges will result in you paying fees of $420160.

The truth is the world of finance is rigged. It doesn't exist for your best interests.

Seriously.

For years the peak body for financial planners, the Financial Planning Association, fought tooth and nail against laws that made advisors act in their clients' best interests. So if they don't want to work in their clients' best interests, whose best interests do you think they're working in?

So what's the solution?

Tinder.

Those of you who are married may not know of Tinder (although 43 per cent of Tinder users *are* married, so that blows that theory). Anyway, Tinder is a rapidfire hookup (as opposed to dating) app.

Most people don't go on Tinder looking for the love of their life.

It's totally...transactional.

People are very clear about what they're looking for (swipe right) and what they're not (swipe left).

While I probably wouldn't recommend this for finding you the love of your life, it's exactly how you should approach hiring a professional advisor.

Find your financial advisor the Tinder way

Don't get me wrong.

While you should never give up financial control, there are times that you need the guidance of an expert advisor.

However, as with Tinder, that doesn't mean you need to shack up and share your assets with them for the rest of your life. It simply means getting the job done and movin' on.

On the farm we have a saying: 'right person, right job'.

You don't get the fencer to do the shearing, and you don't get the shearer to cut your hair (actually, it is pretty much the same thing…I mean it's all just hair right? Though my wife doesn't agree.)

When it comes to getting expert advice, the same rules apply.

The Barefoot Steps will get you 80 per cent of the way there, and the following people will get you over the line. Even better, some of the most knowledgeable, independent, helpful people in this industry don't charge you for their services. Crazy, huh? Let's get swiping.

- **If you're in over your head and can't pay your debts…**

    Call the National Debt Helpline on 1800 007 007 and talk to or set up an appointment with a community based, not-for-profit financial counsellor. They're free, they're confidential and they're the unsung heroes of the financial world. I like them so much, I'm donating 10 per cent of my royalties from this book to their peak body, Financial Counselling Australia.

- **If you need help setting up and maximising your age pension…**

    Call Centrelink on 132 300 and arrange a face-to-face meeting with one of their Financial Information Service Officers (FISOs). They can help you sort out your Centrelink entitlements and also give you unbiased general retirement planning advice that lays out your options without the hard sell. The service is free and independent—and it rocks.

- **If you need help with your super…**

    Call your super fund. They'll have financial advisors who can help you plan your retirement. Your first meeting with them should be both fee-free and obligation-free. Thereafter they'll charge you an hourly fee. Just like your plumber does.

- **If you need help to buy some shares...**

Contact your bank. They'll have a share trading service, or they'll refer you to one. Buying and selling shares is simple: think of it as a mix of internet banking and eBay. You can even buy shares over the phone with an operator once you've set up your account.

If you want some advice on which stocks to buy, you have two choices: head over to asx.com.au, where you can search for a 'full-service broker'—that is, someone who'll recommend stocks. Alternatively (blatant plug alert), you can join our Barefoot Blueprint investment newsletter.

- **If you need help sorting out aged-care options...**

Again, call Centrelink on 132 300 and arrange a face-to-face meeting with one of their FISOs. The service is free and unbiased. They'll explain the costs involved with aged care, impacts on the age pension, options with your former home and estate planning considerations. What have you got to lose?

- **If you need help sorting out your insurance...**

Again, call your super fund. They'll have financial advisors who can do a risk assessment and recommend insurance both inside and outside of super—and at wholesale rates instead of the eye-gouging commissions most financial planners charge (up to 125 per cent of the first year's premium—now that's what I call eye-gouging). Again, you'll pay an hourly fee for this service, and remember, you have my scripts on page 39.

- **If you need a will drawn up...**

You could get a will kit from the newsagent, which is perfectly legal. But there's a good chance you could stuff it up. Instead, I'd strongly suggest you make an appointment with a professional at State Trustees and get them to draw up a legal will and an 'enduring power of attorney'.

They've done more wills than you've had hot dates. It'll cost you about $400. My only bit of advice here would be to **NOT** make them the executor of your will (for that, choose your most reliable family member or friend).

Here are their digits:

ACT: (02) 6207 9800, ptg.act.gov.au

NSW: 1300 364 103, tag.nsw.gov.au

NT: (08) 8999 7271, nt.gov.au/law/bdm/about-public-trustee

Queensland: 1300 360 044, pt.qld.gov.au

South Australia: (08) 8226 9200, publictrustee.sa.gov.au

Tasmania: 1800 068 784, publictrustee.tas.gov.au

Victoria: 1300 138 672, statetrustees.com.au

Western Australia: 1300 746 116, publictrustee.wa.gov.au

And if life's a bit more, shall we say, 'Geoffrey Edelsten' (read blended families, lots of dough), you should go to the Law Institute website in your state and find a solicitor who's an expert in professional estate planning.

- **If you need a home loan...**

If you're refinancing, it's probably easier to bitch than it is to switch. Follow my scripts on page 202 and prepare to save a fortune.

If you're going for your first home, check out online players like UBank and ING, who generally have the cheapest rates (although you'll need to have a 20 per cent deposit and a solid savings history).

If you have multiple properties or a non-standard situation, call a cash-back mortgage broker like Mates Rates on 1300 558 161, who'll refund you the annual trailing commission the banks pay them. It can be as much as $1000 a year, every year, on a $500 000 mortgage.

- **If you need an accountant...**

If you're a business owner, an accountant can be invaluable. Same if you have complicated tax structures like family trusts. But if you're an average wage earner, don't bother—use the ATO's myTax instead. Access it through your myGov account. With myTax you can do your return online—in around five minutes—because the system pre-fills your information. So all you need to do is double-check the info, enter any deductions, hit 'submit' and save yourself the $400 you'd pay to a tax agent to do basically the same thing.

But what about those deductions? Well, the ATO app has a tool for that too. It's called myDeductions, and it's actually pretty good. It allows you to take photos of receipts and enter work-related deductions on the fly. If you're claiming a car expense, it has a built-in GPS tracker to record car trips. Best of all, it feeds directly into myTax.

The bottom line is that the ATO operates under a self-reporting system, which means it's up to you what you put on your tax return. But don't try to fool them—the ATO's supercomputer collects data on 650 million separate transactions by cross-referencing bank accounts, share certificates, Centrelink payments and more.

What to do if you've already got an advisor

What about if you've already got an advisor who's fondling your assets and showing you his pie chart?

Well, it's time to have 'the talk'.

Actually we're Aussies and we don't like confrontation. So take the passive aggressive approach by sending them this email—and blame me.

Dear (advisor's name)

I've decided to do a review of my finances.

Could you please do the following three things for me:

1. Print me a statement that clearly shows my annual percentage return since we began, net of fees.

2. Benchmark my return against the relevant accumulation index for the same period.

3. Provide me with an itemised list of fees (expressed in both dollars and percentages). Include any and all ongoing fees, commissions and administrative costs that I'm charged.

Kind regards,

Be warned, though.

If you send this email—and over the years I've suggested to thousands of people to do it—you can't put the genie back in the bottle. When you see in black and white how much you've paid over the years, you'll become a raging Tinder swinger.

Be dumb smart

One of our biggest fears is looking dumb in front of others, and experts can use that against you—whether that be a mechanic, a doctor or a financial planner.

However, some of the smartest and wealthiest people I know spend most of their time looking dumb.

Case in point, one of the wealthiest investors I know has a standard line when he's looking at a deal:

'You'll have to take it slowly with me; I'm kind of simple.'

When you're dealing with anyone regarding money, you should ask lots of dumb questions until you get the answers you want. You're in control. It's your money. And if you get the feeling someone doesn't have your best interests at heart, or you're just getting a bad vibe—walk away.

Always trust your gut.

It's not about you— a gift for your family

The day our house burned down, I remember looking into my wife's eyes and seeing how devastated she was. It's the closest I'll ever get to being able to hover over her—Patrick Swayze ghost like—and watch her deal with my death. (And given she's younger, fitter and a much safer driver than me, it's likely I'll be going to the great toaster in the sky long before she does.)

Every day a wife, a husband or a partner loses a loved one.

Eventually, it will happen to your family—and possibly when you least expect it. At that moment, the most loving thing you can do for them is the simple, unselfish act I'm about to share with you.

Now, I understand you're probably not going to want to do this. So I'm going to make it ridiculously simple for you. Go to Officeworks and buy a folder and some plastic pockets. Over the next month, as you pay your bills, create the following tabs:

- *Advisors*: Write down the contact details of your accountant, lawyer, financial planner, stockbroker or other professionals you've met on Tinder.

- *Bank accounts*: Include account details and passwords for any account related to you with any money in it, and any outstanding loans you have.

- *Investments*: Print off your latest share portfolio (including share registry details), your managed fund holdings, your superannuation account details (along with your binding nomination, which tells your fund who gets your super) and titles to any properties you hold.

- *Insurance policies*: Include all your policies, using a highlighter to circle the policy numbers and relevant telephone numbers.
- *Funeral instructions*: I want Dire Straits' 'Money for Nothing' to play at my funeral. I also want to go cheap on the burial but expensive on the booze. Your ideas may be different. Write them down.
- *Personal documents*: Include your birth certificate and marriage certificate(s), and copies of your driver's licence, passport, Medicare card and any other important stuff.
- *Passwords*: This is a big one. Facebook, Twitter, email, Tinder and whatever else you have. Just make sure everything's there so they can be shut down.
- *Up-to-date will*: Remember to include the name of your executor and your enduring power of attorney.
- A video of your parents (this one's for my wife, Liz).

About this last one, my wife's father died a few years before I met her. And in the fire we lost some of the last remaining photos of him, the letters he'd written and the paintings he cherished. Her physical reminders are now lost in the ashes.

So how does my wife explain to me who her father was?

How does she explain to our sons who grandpa was?

If you're lucky enough to have your parents still with you, here's how to maintain their legacy.

Whip out your phone, hit 'record' and ask your parents (together or separately) the following:

1. How did you meet?
2. What does being a parent mean to you?
3. What are you most proud of?
4. What advice can you share with me about money, life and happiness?
5. How would you like to be remembered?

This is not for Facebook or Snapchat.

It's for your and your family's legacy. One day, it's all you'll have left of them.

And you'll treasure it.

Once you've finished putting together the folder, there are only a few things left to do.

Find a safe place to store it (I'd suggest paying for a safety deposit box—houses can burn down).

Then write a letter to your spouse and your kids. Tell them you love them.

This is a good warm-up to the ninth, and final, Barefoot Step...

We rescued our retirement!

Ted and Rita Turnour, QLD

Five years ago, we had $40 000 and no shares. Now, we're aiming at hitting seven figures in the next few years.

We were small business owners when the GFC hit. Everything was imploding and we were burning serious money in our business. We were not really in control of our future and we hated that.

We didn't have much but we were determined to be self-sufficient in retirement. We just didn't trust financial advice from anybody, and shares—we thought they were a lottery. Looking back, we lived week to week without knowing what we needed to do.

Then we started reading Barefoot.

It was a winner, as far as we were concerned. We worked our way through all your commentaries and calculators.

Control your own finances (tread your own path) was the big message and we loved it. We read everything you have written and started to organise our finances around your advice.

Five years ago, we had $40 000 and no shares. Now, we have amassed $250 000 in investments with the aim of seven figures in the next few years.

We have stopped worrying about the future.

We have a lot of spare cash in the bank for the first time ever, a nice Mojo account for a rainy day and a nice bevy of shares in super and some property. Our finances have never been in better shape. If we want to go somewhere or stay somewhere, money is the last issue, which is a wonderful change.

We recommend Barefoot to everybody. If money comes up, my mantra is, 'read *The Barefoot Investor*'. Family, friends, employees, the local cafe owner … you name it and we would recommend Barefoot to it!

Dear Barefoot Team, be very proud of Scott. He has done the Australian community a great service with the Barefoot Investor.

Thousands of people have great faith in their future because of you and your advice. Sometimes it's so corny, sometimes it's a valve bleed, sometimes it grates like chalk on a blackboard, but the inherent truth of your guidance is read and acted upon. I thank you for my lightbulb moment and for having the balls to say no to the big end of town.

We would never have had that confidence to do this without your lead.

I'm laughing as I write and very happily treading my own path.

STEP 9

LEAVE A LEGACY

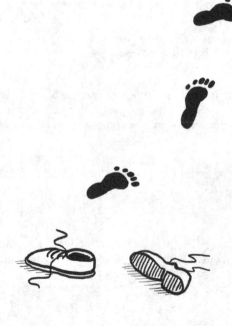

Each of the Barefoot Steps has moved you along the path to financial freedom.

You've now reached the final step: 'Leave a Legacy'.

Now you may be thinking, 'hey there's no mathematics here—where's the finance, bro?'

Listen: there are plenty of wealthy people who are miserable sacks of... stocks. Seriously, why bother gaining control of your money and your life if you don't use it to put a smile on your dial?

Let me call a spade a bloody shovel: you are going to die.

There will be a funeral for you, and there will be people who stand up and talk about you.

What will they say?

More importantly, what would you like them to say?

Well, Step 9 is all about giving them something to talk about.

And that's what this step's Date Night is all about.

Building your legacy—a very special Barefoot Date Night

Liz and I still do our monthly Barefoot Date Night, even though our financial life is pretty well sorted.

While we still talk about our investments and keep track of our buckets, we also talk about more meaningful stuff—like how we can spend our time and our money in a way that makes us proud.

If you follow the Barefoot Steps, you'll eventually become wealthy. I have absolutely no doubt about it. It'll work for you, just as it has for the people you've read about in this book—and for the thousands of Barefooters who write to me every year.

However, for some people, the only thing they gain from money is the fear of losing it. They get so caught up in the game, they never work out if they're winning. They never ask 'How much is enough?', and they continue spending their time in jobs they don't like, to buy ever more expensive things to impress people they don't like.

So on this last Barefoot Date Night (well, it's the last one in this book, though your own should continue on), you're going to look at your legacy.

Leave your phone at home.

Unplug from the face-suck of the glowing screen.

For one evening, you'll stop gawking at other people and think about your life.

How will you be remembered?

At your funeral, they won't say:

'He drove a C-Class Mercedes … the limited edition … the one with the *quilted* trim.'

No, they'll talk about the good things you did, and the difference you made to those you loved.

Don't get me wrong, it doesn't need to be Bill Gates grand. You don't need to have a building named after you, or have cured poverty, or hold any world records.

When my grandfather died, three generations of his family held hands and stood around his grave. Then they played (what has become my favourite song of all time) 'The Man in the Picture' by The Bobkatz:

> That man in the picture, he didn't fly through the air, he's no superhero, he's sure no millionaire. He didn't walk on the moon, he didn't save the world today … but he's my hero anyway. A kind and gentle man, the best friend I ever had, he's my hero … he's my dad.

What do you want to be remembered for? What do you stand for?

These are the meaty things for your Barefoot Date Night.

Give your money

Chennupati Jagadish is one of Australia's leading scientists. Yet he grew up dirt poor in a small village in southern India. In fact, he might never have gone to high school if it weren't for a kind teacher who invited him to live with his family and study.

Now, there are plenty of people who get to the top of the tree only to forget the kind people who helped them along.

Not Chennupati.

He's responsible for helping nearly 1000 women in the third world pull themselves out of poverty, despite being on an academic's wage.

How?

Via an outfit called kiva.org, which he found out about through being a Barefooter.

Kiva (which means 'unity' in Swahili) is an award-winning, not-for-profit website that allows you to make micro-loans (starting at $25) directly to some of the world's poorest entrepreneurs. They, in turn, use the money to start a business, and in the process often pull themselves (and their families) out of poverty.

Kiva provides regular updates on how the entrepreneurs are progressing (an impressive 98.7 per cent of loans are repaid in full). And it's in these updates that you get to form a connection with the people you're helping, and you get to see how $25 changes someone's life.

The Barefoot Investor has its own Kiva lending team, which you can join. So far we've lent out over $500 000 and changed thousands of lives! You can join Chennupati and thousands of others by typing this address into your search bar: www.kiva.org/team/thebarefootinvestor.

Give your time and your money

'What am I going to do now?' said Helen Brown, a stay-at-home mum, after her final son left the nest.

Helen isn't a wealthy woman. She lives in Kyabram, in country Victoria, and her husband runs a small signwriting business.

In 2007 they had their first ever trip overseas—to Uganda. She was struck by the poverty of the people in a village they saw called Lubanda. The following year, she saved up and took two of her sons to the village to meet the women.

The trip was a turning point for Helen and the people of Lubanda. When she returned home she started HUG (Help Us Grow) as a not-for-profit organisation and began fundraising to help the village community help themselves.

Helen is not religious; she just believes passionately in a hand up rather than a handout, and she doesn't draw a wage from HUG. 'Every last cent goes to the community,' she says.

Small chickens?

Hardly.

Since 2008, HUG has built a community centre for the village where the locals come together and learn new skills, as well as a secondary school and a medical clinic that serves a population of around 50000.

How's that for a legacy?

'Why do you do it?' I asked her.

'Because it fills me with absolute joy.'

The digger giving back

Anthony, NSW

The legacy I'd like to leave is to provide financial support to wounded veterans.

I'm a ground defence officer in the Air Force.

I was living on base for three years, and in that time saved up $30000. I was looking at how to invest my money when I found Scott and the Barefoot Blueprint. But before I could start investing I got tapped on the shoulder.

'You're going to Afghanistan.'

I saved $80000 while I was on deployment, and I spent my downtime reading up on the Blueprint. When I came home I made my first share investment. I then diversified into other companies.

In four years, I turned $110000 into $220000.

I don't have any drive to be rich; I only want to be financially secure. In the military we have this saying: 'Don't jack on your mates', which basically means don't be selfish. That's been embedded in my personality.

When you go overseas on assignment it's like the world is not so romantic anymore. You can go one of two ways—grow from the experience or go downhill. There are 11 people I know who've taken their own lives. My father was a train driver and he faced three suicides (people jumping in front of the train), and now has PTSD as a result.

So that's my main driver for giving back—for trying to make a difference.

I thought, wouldn't it be good if someone started a business that took something we do every day and made it meaningful.

So I started 'Brother Shave'.

The idea was simple: the military requires people to shave daily. But razors are expensive and the money we spend on them is huge. So I created a company that provides high-quality razors for a cheaper price, delivered direct to the troops.

We donate $1 per pack to Soldier On, a charity that helps men and women who've been wounded either physically or mentally during service.

The business is going well—I've even been able to employ my dad, who hadn't been able to work due to the PTSD. It gives him purpose and allows us to work together.

The biggest thing I got from Scott was understanding that small amounts of money, saved over a long period, can make a massive difference.

The legacy I'd like to leave is to provide financial support to wounded veterans. And over the long term, my hope is to employ veterans who otherwise can't work due to their injuries (much like my father).

And, I'm proud to say, we're on our way.

The comments from Anthony are his only and do not necessarily reflect the views of the Australian Defence Force.

Recap of Part 3: Harvest

Normal people walk around in a fog of financial fear and indecision.

They worry about losing their jobs, or paying off their debts, or how they'll ever afford to retire.

Not you.

You're no longer 'normal'.

You now have clarity. You're following a time-tested plan that is propelling you towards safety and security. And you're one of the very few people in this country who's getting fiercely independent advice.

You have:

> called your bank, and you're now on track to save $77 641 in interest and wipe almost seven years from your mortgage. Even better, you'll soon have the banker off your back.

> seen exactly what a comfortable retirement looks like ... and you've worked out your individual retirement number, and now you're armed with a bulletproof strategy on how to nail your number.

> got the phone numbers of independent financial experts who can genuinely help you ... rather than sell you some expensive product.

> made a commitment to managing the most precious resource you have—your time—to create a legacy that will live long after you're gone.

Right now you're that girl hugging her father on the Tattslotto ad ... wouldn't it be nice?

You betcha.

You've achieved something that millions of people believe is impossible for them: you'll never ever worry about money again. You're in charge. You call the shots. You're free. You've hit the jackpot!

Enjoy your long, golden harvest!

Prove them wrong

Barbara Hansen, VIC

As he left he said...'You will never survive financially without me'.

When my ex-husband left, he said, 'You will never survive financially without me'.

And for a long time I did struggle.

I was a single parent trying to raise two kids. I had to take a hardship application out on my home loan, because they were pushing for me to do a voluntary default (I fought them off). I had no savings and my only income was from Centrelink.

When you've been in an emotionally abusive relationship, it takes a long time to get that person out of your head.

Then I met my new partner, Geoff, in 2014. Every Sunday he'd read the Barefoot Investor newspaper column, and it's part of our Sunday breakfast ritual. Scott's like a little voice on my shoulder—I've even begun to quote him!

I've become part of the 'Barefoot family' and use the strategies and advice to build my wealth. Before, I'd never even read my super statements; now I actively look at my returns.

Things I couldn't do before, I can do now—I've got $70000 in Mojo! I've even helped my daughter buy a car, and I'm helping my son start a business.

At last I feel free of the noose around my neck. I've stopped burying my head in the sand. Even at my age, you can make a difference to your future. You can't let your past define your future. It's not too late to build wealth.

I have survived financially and I will continue to grow financially because I'm not afraid anymore to take control. I have grabbed my finances by the horns and will never let them go.

Freedom starts today—you don't have to wait...

You and I have come a long way.

Right now you might be feeling that you've got a long stretch ahead of you before you can achieve the same success that others who've followed the Barefoot Steps have achieved.

But the truth is, you're closer than you think.

The truth is, your freedom starts today.

Don't believe me?

Well, let's look at what the hard research suggests: the nation's longest running and most comprehensive survey on happiness, the Australian Unity Wellbeing Index. After 15 years of detailed research, the author of the survey, Deakin University Emeritus Professor Bob Cummins, says he's finally cracked the code to wellbeing, which he has dubbed the 'golden triangle of happiness':

1. A sense of purpose
2. Strong personal relationship/s
3. Financial control.

Let's take a look at each of these.

A sense of purpose

Yes, that sounds like something Malcolm Turnbull would say.

For most people their 'purpose' is pretty simple: to live a better life and to look after their family.

That explains why most people (often unconsciously, with the help of advertisers) strive towards outward symbols of success: owning an expensive home, in an expensive suburb, and driving an expensive car to drop the kids off at an expensive school.

Yet 15 years of detailed research proves—quite convincingly—that once you earn over $70000 a year, money won't make you much happier.

> **Here's you:** What a load of rubbish. I like buying stuff. I'll take the short-term sugar hit!
>
> **Here's me:** It's often what you have to give up to get the sugar hit that makes even high-earning people unhappy. You bite off more than you can chew. You work more. You stress more. You fight more. Ask yourself: is it really worth it?

Strong personal relationship/s

One of the building blocks of happiness is strong personal relationships...yet the number-one cause of relationship break-ups is fighting about money. It's important to understand that Relationships Australia says this is universal, and not just confined to low-income couples who shop at The Reject Shop.

Yet I'm not Doctor Phil, so let's look at something I do understand: money.

Financial security

Money may not make you happy, but the research shows that not being in control of your finances will make you very unhappy: in fact, as I said earlier, Professor Cummins and his research team found that financial insecurity produces similar feelings to those of physical torture.

His survey found that low-income earners who rated themselves at least an 8 out of 10 for being in control of their finances were far happier than those people who were earning substantially more but rated themselves as not as in control of their finances.

Years ago, a woman in her 40s approached me after I gave a seminar in Perth.

Her husband had walked out on her—and their two preschool kids—a few years before. He'd left her with massive debts that he was never going to repay. And she was ... absolutely beaming with happiness.

A friend of hers had given her my book. After she read it, she didn't have any doubts. It was clear to her that if she followed the simple, commonsense plan, she'd be okay. For her there was no doubt. No indecision. She had a roadmap that clearly pointed out her destination. That was enough for her to be able to confidently look herself in the mirror and say, 'I've got this'.

There's science to back this up.

Achieving a sense of financial control isn't about your net worth—it's about your self-worth.

You don't have to wait until you've paid off all your credit cards.

You don't have to wait until you've bought a home.

You don't have to wait until you've paid off your home.

You don't have to wait until you've saved enough for retirement.

You don't have to wait for *anything*.

You achieve the freedom of control the very moment you make the decision to commit to following a commonsense plan. A plan that's realistic and based on hard work, saving, paying down debt and investing. When you know in your bones it will work, your anxiety will vanish immediately. It then becomes a matter of time: so long as you keep following the plan, everything will be okay.

You can be in control of your money right now, regardless of your situation.

You now have a plan. It's been tested on thousands of people over many years.

And it works.

So let's look at it one last time.

THE BAREFOOT STEPS
ON ONE PAGE

STEP 1
SCHEDULE A MONTHLY
BAREFOOT DATE NIGHT

STEP 2
SET UP YOUR
BUCKETS

STEP 3
DOMINO YOUR
DEBTS

STEP 4
BUY YOUR HOME

STEP 5
INCREASE YOUR SUPER
TO 15 PER CENT

STEP 6
BOOST YOUR MOJO
TO THREE MONTHS

STEP 7
GET THE BANKER
OFF YOUR BACK

STEP 8
NAIL YOUR
RETIREMENT
NUMBER

STEP 9
LEAVE A LEGACY

We'll meet again

You've probably had someone in your past who doubted you.

Someone who told you that you couldn't do it, and that you 'shouldn't get ahead of yourself'.

It may have been your dad; it could have been a teacher, or an old boss; and it almost certainly came from your biggest critic: the person who stares back in the mirror at you each morning.

But you will win.

Like the rest of the Barefooters you've read about in this book, if you follow the Barefoot Steps that I've laid out for you, your success is guaranteed.

Here's what's going to happen. A year from now I'll be sitting in the sunshine on the verandah at my farm, looking out over the green hills that were once black and burnt.

I'll fire up my laptop, open my inbox and click on the email you've just sent me (scott@barefootinvestor.com).

You'll tell me about the steps you've taken, about your Barefoot Date Nights, and about your planting, growing and harvesting... and how deeply proud you are of yourself.

And I'll call Liz over and read lines from your email to her, and we'll marvel at just how far you've come in such a short time.

Till then...

From this point on, no matter what you face in the future, you can now look yourself in the eye and confidently say to yourself...

I've got this

A final word

Most days I help someone, somewhere, who's fighting their own financial fire.

It could be a young father who has terminal cancer. A teenager with out-of-control credit card debts. An elderly pensioner who can't afford to turn on the heater. A widow with young kids. A family who are about to have their home repossessed.

Everyone needs a helping hand occasionally.

After the fire, I needed help myself.

And in the fog of those first few days my most cherished memory is of Liz coming back from the post office with one of their postal trolleys loaded to the brim with gifts and letters from people all over the country. We received thousands of letters and emails. Our son was sent more toys than Richie Rich.

This book is my way of paying it forward.

It's everything I've learned from the decade or so that I've been helping people with their money.

It's everything I've learned from losing the lot and having to start from scratch.

And it's everything you need to be prepared for when you face your financial fire.

Now, I have a favour to ask of you.

If you got anything out of this book—if you highlighted or circled anything—please pay it forward and give this book to someone else. Ask them to read it. They need your help to get prepared for their financial fire.

Spread the word.

Are You Ready to Take the Next Step?

Okay, you've read the book.

You're excited. You're ready to take control of your money, right?

Well, you don't have to do it all on your own.

The truth is, if you hang around people who are on the same path, you'll not only get there quicker—you'll have more fun too!

When I started out I didn't have any support structure—people I could talk to about my goals and not be judged, and who would keep me on track. So I created it.

It's called the *Barefoot Blueprint*, and it's one of Australia's fastest growing investment newsletters.

Each month I give fiercely independent investment recommendations to my members and I show them in real time how I invest $100 000 of my own money.

Yet it's much more than that.

The *Barefoot Blueprint* is a living, breathing community.

It's made up of thousands of Barefooters of all ages, all income levels, and all experience levels (some total investment novices, others seasoned pros).

What brings us together is that we're all treading our own path.

There are social meet-ups around the country and online, and there are thousands of supportive posts in our private community.

The Blueprint is my labour of love ... it's where I direct 90 per cent of my efforts, answering members' questions and guiding them to their goals.

So if you'd like to be the newest member of our community, head over to BarefootInvestor.com.

Tread Your Own Path!

Index